SCRIPTURE
ALONE

BHP BOOKS BY JAMES R. WHITE

The Forgotten Trinity
The God Who Justifies
Grieving: Our Path Back to Peace
The King James Only Controversy
Mary—Another Redeemer?
The Roman Catholic Controversy
The Same Sex Controversy*
Scripture Alone

*with Jeffrey Dean Niell

SCRIPTURE ALONE

JAMES R. WHITE

Minneapolis, Minnesota

Published by Bethany House Publishers
11400 Hampshire Avenue South
Bloomington, Minnesota 55438

Bethany House Publishers is a division of
Baker Publishing Group, Grand Rapids, Michigan.

Printed in the United States of America

Library of Congress Cataloging-in-Publication Data

White, James R. (James Robert), 1962-
    Scripture alone : exploring the Bible's accuracy, authority, and authenticity / by James R. White.
        p. cm.
    ISBN 0-7642-2048-9 (pbk.)
    1. Bible—Evidences, authority, etc. I. Title.
    BS480.W489   2004
    220.1—dc22   2004012911

This book is dedicated to my son,

Joshua Daniel White.

I have often said God knew I could never pursue the ministry He has entrusted to me without giving me the best children He had available, and so He did. My son is a great source of joy and fulfillment, and I openly and gladly tell any who wish to hear that I could never pursue this work without the support of my wife, my son, and my daughter. The defender of the faith in these pages is named Joshua in honor of my son and of my having had the tremendous privilege of baptizing him at the Phoenix Reformed Baptist Church, where I am an elder. Thank you, Joshua, my son and also my brother in Christ.

JAMES WHITE is the author of several acclaimed books, including *The King James Only Controversy* and *The Forgotten Trinity*. He is an elder of the Phoenix Reformed Baptist Church, director of Alpha and Omega Ministries—a Christian apologetics organization, an adjunct professor with Golden Gate Baptist Theological Seminary, and professor of apologetics with Columbia Evangelical Seminary. He and his family live in Phoenix.

Contents

Introduction

Every author thinks his or her book is truly *needed* at his or her time in church history. At least I like to think so. I would hate to think anyone writes books just for the sake of writing books. I certainly do not: Every editor with whom I've ever worked will testify that I often comment on having no intention to reinvent the wheel. I have not written a book specifically on Jehovah's Witnesses, for example, simply because there are a number of very good works already in print on the subject, written by solid authors and containing solid information. Why should I repeat what someone else has already done?

However, the book you hold in your hands, if God has blessed my efforts in writing it, is unlike any other book currently available. Sure, every book is unique, but I mean this in a particular sense. And yes, any book I write will be unique because of my background, which includes more than four dozen moderated public debates against leading apologists of prominent religious beliefs (almost all of whom are united in denying the sufficiency of the Bible to function as the church's sole infallible rule of faith); seminary teaching experience in the biblical languages, apologetics, and theology; and the office of elder in a local Christ-professing, Bible-believing church.[1] *Scripture Alone* should be specifically unique because of what I am seeking to do and because of the impact I want it to have upon you, the reader.

First, I am not seeking to write a massive scholarly tome on *sola scriptura*. That has already been done more than once,[2] and tremendous works defending this truth are already in print. This book should be considered a primer, an introduction, to those much longer works. In general, the great works of past believers are not written in a popular style; they spoke more clearly to past generations. One must *want* to work through them to arrive at the goal, and it is my intention to compel my fellow believers to *want* to do that work.

Second, I write as a pastor/theologian/apologist who believes firmly that man is a singular whole—you cannot divide man's mind from his heart, his soul. I am passionate about theology, passionate about the faith. I honestly do not understand how anyone can say "I believe the Bible is the Word of God" without being *passionate* about that confession. I love the Trinity, justification by faith, the Resurrection, and *sola scriptura*. I do not pretend to be dispassionate about these things, and, as such, I stand firmly on this assertion: Christian scholarship that lacks passion about the truth is not worthy of the name *Christian* to begin with. If dispassion and detachment are necessary attributes of scholarship, then I do not seek the appellation. I cannot comprehend dry faith, arid confession, or mere mental assent. A person who has only intellectual knowledge of the sufficiency of Scripture, but lacks a deep, abiding love of the Scriptures and an understanding of how their sufficiency is related to the gospel and to the assurance of salvation, is liable to be led astray by winsome words or the traditions of men. At the same time, a person who professes great zeal for the truth, but does not honor the truth by growing in knowledge of it, can be easily led astray. We need a balanced understanding of and love

---

[1]Phoenix Reformed Baptist Church, Phoenix, Arizona *(www.prbc.org)*.
[2]See below, under "On the Backs of Giants."

for the truth of *sola scriptura*. Divine truths command our undivided allegiance, and this love of divine truth is what I seek to encourage in your heart.

ON THE BACKS OF GIANTS

I have always believed in *sola scriptura*, though the Latin phrase did not enter into my vocabulary until adulthood. When I first began responding to attacks made upon Scripture by various religious groups, I did so out of instinctual respect for the Bible and a strong sense of loyalty to the Word. Even in my conservative Bible college, little was said about the doctrine; it was simply assumed. I was blissfully unaware of the tremendous effort that had been expended in the defense of Scripture's sufficiency by God's people in past generations.

The Reformation, traditionally dated as beginning with the posting of Luther's Ninety-five Theses on October 31, 1517, brought intense focus to the issue of scriptural sufficiency. Indeed, the formal principle of the Reformation was *sola scriptura*, for it was the assertion of biblical sufficiency over against tradition that allowed for the recovery of certain biblical doctrines: justification by grace through faith alone, the proper form and governance of the church, the individual priesthood of the believer, and much more. The preeminence of the Word can be seen in Luther's comment:

> The Word comes first, and with the Word the Spirit breathes upon my heart so that I believe.[3]

Rome taught that because she was the custodian of sacred tradition, people needed her magisterial authority; hence, Rome vehemently opposed and denied the idea of Scripture alone as the sole infallible rule of faith for the church. Neither did Rome sit quietly in response to the Reformation, as the Catholic counterreformation blossomed in the latter decades of the sixteenth century. The chief ecclesiastical manifestation of this movement was the Council of Trent (1546–1564), which

---

[3]Martin Luther, *Luther's Works,* Vol. 54 : *Table Talk* (Augsburg Fortress, 1999, [c] 1967).

began its work by issuing a declaration on the issue of the nature of Scripture itself (April 1546). The council not only claimed authority to define the extent of the canon but also sought to "check unbridled spirits" (i.e., those who refused to acknowledge the ultimate authority of the papacy), decreeing,

> No one relying on his own judgment shall, in matters of faith and morals pertaining to the edification of Christian doctrine, distorting the Holy Scriptures in accordance with his own conceptions, presume to interpret them contrary to that sense which holy mother Church, to whom it belongs to judge of their true sense and interpretation, has held and holds, or even contrary to the unanimous teaching of the Fathers, even though such interpretations should never at any time be published.[4]

Just how all-encompassing Rome's authority claims were (and are) can be perceived by listening to the words of a leading counterreformation figure, the founder of the Jesuit order (The Society of Jesus), Ignatius Loyola. He taught his followers: "That we may be altogether of the same mind and in conformity with the Church herself, if she shall have defined anything to be black which to our eyes appears to be white, we ought in like manner to pronounce it black."[5]

This is supremacy of the church over the Scriptures with a vengeance; Loyola sent out legions of like-minded men to "take back for mother church" what had once been hers. The battle was joined, and while Calvin and Luther had discussed the issue of scriptural sufficiency in their writings, it would be left to their heirs to continue the conflict with the counter-reformation. One of the first to provide a substantive response was Lutheran Martin Chemnitz, whose *Examination of the Council of Trent* takes up four hardbound volumes in its current publication. Coming right on the heels of the council, it was a

---

[4]Heinrich Denzinger, *The Sources of Catholic Dogma* (Herder, 1957), 786.
[5]St. Ignatius Loyola, "Rules for Thinking With the Church," Rule 13 (cited from *Documents of the Christian Church*, ed., Henry Bettenson [Oxford University Press, 1947] 364–65).

timely response that still carries value.[6]

The two most useful works from the era following the Reformation were penned by William Whitaker and Francis Turretin. Whitaker's *Disputation on Holy Scripture: Against the Papists* first appeared in 1588; recently republished (but only briefly in print), this work is still available in major libraries and is well worth the effort to obtain and read. Likewise, Turretin's *Institutes of Elenctic Theology* has been recently republished[7] and is valuable not only for its defense of biblical sufficiency but also for its wide-ranging scope and depth of learning.

Even so, disputes arise with each generation, and the great "Tractarian Movement" (or "Oxford Movement") in nineteenth-century England called forth one of the greatest defenses of biblical sufficiency ever penned. William Goode's *Divine Rule of Faith and Practice* first emerged in 1842, then was expanded and published in three volumes in 1853. Goode's work broke ground in providing a more modern response to those who had developed new arguments designed to subjugate Scripture to an external authority. As has always seemed to be the case with the enemies of *sola scriptura,* the primary response was silence—the "if we ignore it, it may go away" style of apologetic. And in some ways this has worked, as the vast majority of believers today have never heard of Whitaker or Goode.

A few decades later another important (though less in-depth) work was released: George Salmon's *The Infallibility of the Church.*[8] Finally, the most recent turn of the century brought one of the lengthiest defenses of *sola scriptura,* and in the manner of Goode and Salmon, this new work speaks to the generation in which it is birthed (each generation invents new ways of packaging error). David King and William Webster have written *Holy Scripture: The Ground and Pillar of Our Faith,*[9] which

[6]Martin Chemnitz, *Examination of the Council of Trent,* trans., Fred Kramer (Concordia Publishing House, 1986). At times it is difficult to follow Chemnitz's references, especially since the more standardized divisions of the early church writings had not yet been introduced.
[7]Francis Turretin, *Institutes of Elenctic Theology,* trans., George Giger, ed., James Dennison, Jr. (Presbyterian and Reformed, 1992).
[8]George Salmon, *The Infallibility of the Church* (Baker, 1959). This work has been republished and can be obtained in libraries as well.
[9]David T. King and William A. Webster, *Holy Scripture: The Ground and Pillar of Our Faith,* 3 vols. (Christian Resources, 2001).

provides a modern response to the resurgence of Catholic apologetics and the recycling of arguments long ago refuted (by Calvin or Whitaker or Goode) but put forward yet again in the service of the Roman Church.

The advent of postmodernism, the enshrinement of Darwinian orthodoxy in the educational systems of Western society, and the rise of blatant humanism as the religion-by-default of large subcultures have brought no end of new challenges to biblical sufficiency. We cannot simply deal with the issues raised by those from other times; now we must honestly evaluate *sola scriptura* in the light of quantum physics, genetic engineering, and nuclear weapons. The task is the same in every generation: *If God's Word is to be heard, we who love it must stand in its defense.*

A WORD ABOUT SCRIPTURE "ALONE"

The title of this work is *Scripture Alone.* Just as the phrase *faith alone* (*sola fide,* the great cry of the Reformation, though no longer the great cry of many who were once considered children of the Reformation) is often misrepresented, so too *Scripture alone* could be misunderstood. When we say that faith alone brings justification, we are not saying that faith should be considered in a vacuum, separated from everything else God does in the work of salvation. Instead, *sola fide* means that faith, apart from any concept of merit or works (actually in opposition thereto), is the sole means of justification. In the same way, *Scripture alone* does not mean that God zoomed by planet earth, dropped off the Scriptures, and left us on our own. As we will note when we define *sola scriptura,* this is not a claim, for instance, that there is no church or that there is no Spirit. The title does not suggest that Scripture, apart from the Spirit, outside the church, is God's only means of leading His people. It *is,* however, saying that Scripture is utterly unique in its nature as God-breathed revelation (nothing else is God-breathed); it is unparalleled and absolute in its authority; and it is the sole infallible rule of faith for the church. It is both a positive statement, asserting the supremacy and uniqueness of the Word, and a negative one, denying the existence of any other rule of authority on the same level. One would be dreadfully misunderstanding this book's title to think it supports the idea of a Christian absenting himself from the body of Christ, rejecting biblical teaching about elders and leaders,[10] and perpetually sitting under a tree somewhere alone with the Bible. While an individual believer may derive great benefit from solitary contemplation of God's truth in such a context, it will always lead one back to service to his or her fellow believers in the church and to ministry within the context of being salt and light in the world.

WHY DIALOGUES?

In some sections of this work I have presented "dialogues," fictional[11] encounters wherein the topic at hand is discussed. I have found over the course of my ministry that great truths of the faith often shine the brightest against the dark backdrop of error. Further, people usually find "listening" to a conversation easier and more interesting to follow. Finally, presenting portions of my defense of *sola scriptura* in dialogue form serves the exceptionally valuable purpose of training believers and preparing them to actually engage in the work of ministry within their own respective callings. There is no reason to learn divine truths if we do not apply them in our hearts and minds, live them out daily, and defend them in the public square when we are given the opportunity to glorify God in so doing. The dialogues found throughout this work are not intended, of course, to provide any kind of programmed system of argumentation. Footnotes provide further information, and, of course, every personal encounter will take its own twists and turns depending upon the other person's personal beliefs, level of understanding, and so on. Nevertheless, through broadly outlined presentations of how these dialogues can be successfully undertaken, the believer can be encouraged to speak out in defense of the truth.

---

[10]See Hebrews 13:7, 17.
[11]Though very much based on my own experience as an apologist.

SO WHY THIS BOOK?

If, then, it is not my intention to repeat the work of Goode, and since I recognize that the challenges to biblical sufficiency go far beyond the post-Reformation debate with Rome, what is my goal? Let me lay it out with clarity right from the start.

This book is a *passionate introduction* to a topic that is foundational to sound, biblical Christianity. It is passionate in that I am convinced that without a solid grasp of this belief, nothing else in the faith will have the essential basis upon which to stand. Consequently, because it is a revealed truth and because it is vital to the spiritual health of Christ's people, I seek to enflame within my fellow believers a strong commitment to this truth, one that cannot be shaken by the "smooth and flattering speech" (Romans 16:18) of the many false teachers circling about the outside of the true flock, seeking those whom they may devour. My delight in *sola scriptura,* and in the truth that Scripture is God speaking to us, is a function of *both* my status as a redeemed man who realizes how utterly dependent I am upon the Spirit of God[12] *and* my calling as a pastor in the local church, which instills within me a concern for the welfare of Christ's sheep. If I accomplish my goal, the reader of this book—if a fellow believer in the Lord Jesus Christ, indwelt by the same Spirit who carried men along as they spoke from God in the Scriptures (2 Peter 1:21)—will have a greater appreciation of this doctrine's vital centrality, a deeper understanding of the issues involved, and a solid commitment to press on in the lifelong study of this foundational truth.

---

[12]It is the Spirit who drives me to the Word He Himself has produced and guarded.

CHAPTER 1

Three Arguments Related to Scriptural Sufficiency

To illustrate the task before us, allow me to present three arguments, all related to our topic. *Notice how each is presented and where it leads.*

ARGUMENT ONE

Man is a creature, a created being of tremendous capacity and ability. Nonetheless, his essential nature is that of a creation, something dependent upon the will and power of another. The Creator has indelibly stamped the creature *man* with an image, a likeness, certain qualities and characteristics that mark him and her out from the rest of the created order on earth. The body of these unique traits and abilities we call the *imago Dei,* the image of God.

While most of God's complex earthly creatures communicate with one another in basic ways, much of this communication is merely instinctual and not definitive of the species. Man, on the other hand, is marked not only by his ability to communicate but also by the near *necessity* of communication. Man was designed to desire interaction with his fellow humans; to deprive him of this is in many ways to deprive him of life itself.

Consider as one example the lengths to which the deaf or the blind go to engage in communication. We regard it as severe punishment to imprison a person in solitary confinement, and almost inhuman punishment to take away all forms of contact with other people. While people communicate in many ways, they interact primarily through language, whether spoken or written; the complexity and capacity of human language testifies to humankind's inherent desire to communicate and relate with others.

It is eminently logical to believe that the God who formed man's body, with all of its intricate biological facilities, who created the wonder of man's mind, with all of its amazing intellectual capacities, and who instilled man's very ability and desire to communicate, would Himself be capable of communication with His creatures. The very thought of a mute God is on its face absurd: The only basis upon which one might suppose God to be silent would be God purposefully choosing to remain so. But even this makes no sense, as if God would create man to be desirous of communication and then absent Himself from the scene so as to leave us wandering alone in the midst of the vast, silent creation. Such a God would hardly be worthy of praise or emulation.

No, God must be able to communicate, and that on a level at least equal to that of His human creatures.[1] Otherwise, from whence would our abilities come? God is able to make Himself known, to communicate His will, His thoughts, and His desires to His creation. This is simply necessary if, in fact, God is the Creator of all that is.

And so we should ask ourselves not *if* God has revealed Himself to man, but *how* and *when*? Again we are struck immediately by the fact that if God is to reveal Himself with clarity, His revelation must be capable of carrying the same kind of "truth content" as our own speech. That is, through the use of

---

[1] I say "at least equal to" simply because it is irrational to assume God could give to His creatures an ability greater than what He Himself possesses. Obviously, I believe God is capable of communicating with far greater clarity and power than His creatures.

context (including grammar, syntax, connotation, et al.) we expect to be able to communicate to another person certain facts. Our society functions on the basis of this truth; while disputes arise regarding the language of contracts and the specificities of meaning, we still assume that given sufficient effort, communication can take place. When we launch exploratory spacecraft we do so believing that the scientists and engineers involved can interrelate with sufficient clarity so as to accomplish the task. Therefore, God must be able to communicate truth to us.

If we combine this line of reasoning with the assumption that God has a purpose in His creation and is pursuing His own ends therein, we can see that God would have a motive to reveal His truths in such a fashion so as to produce the ends He desires. If those ends were to include the clear communication of truths to the whole of humanity or to any specific portion thereof, how might God communicate so as to allow this revelation to serve generations of human beings? Obviously, a written document, or set of documents, transmitted over time would allow for a revelation of transcendent truths.[2] The consistency of the revelation would provide a means of maintaining its integrity over time.[3]

The preceding series of arguments, taken as one whole, is consistent within itself—there are no logical contradictions. Obviously, if God wished to reveal Himself to His creation, He could do so in a written body of revelation. In fact, such a revelation is consistent with the facts of creation as we have experienced them.

ARGUMENT TWO

The divine truth of biblical sufficiency is based firmly upon the bedrock of the nature of Scripture and God's sovereign

---

[2]That God has a purpose in giving His revelation is a part of scriptural revelation, as we will note in chapter 5.

[3]I refer here to the consistency of the revelation itself providing the means (through exegesis) of correcting misinterpretation, not specifically to the transmission of the text. The protection of the text over time falls under God's purpose in giving the revelation in the first place; that is, if God has a purpose in giving the revelation, He will then see to its protection over time.

rule over His creation. That is to say, scriptural sufficiency is not a doctrine unto itself that can be separated from the rest of revelation; it is the *necessary result* of sound beliefs concerning God and His purposes. To believe what the Bible teaches about God, the gospel, the church, and itself is to believe in scriptural sufficiency, the Bible's ability to function as the sole infallible rule of faith for the church and to equip God's people for every good work that God, by His Spirit, would call us to perform. In the words of Scripture, Christ's church hears the voice of her Master.

While numerous elements of the scriptural witness lead us to conclude that the Bible is God's Word, sufficient for the church, two major teachings form the core of this belief: (1) the nature of Scripture, and (2) the Bible's teaching on the only other possible "candidate" for a necessary complement[4] to written divine revelation, that being tradition. These can be summarized as follows.

First, the Bible is God's Word in written form. There can be little question that this is the constant testimony of Scripture itself. From the "Thus saith the Lord" of the prophets to the "It is written" of the apostles, the biblical writers recognize that God has spoken and that the Scriptures record for us His Word. From the ode to God's law in Psalm 119, through the teaching ministry of the Lord Jesus, to the polished confessions of 2 Timothy 3:14–17 and 2 Peter 1:20–21, the message is the same: *God has spoken in His Word.* Paul captures this truth when he describes the Scriptures as "God-breathed," and *nothing else is described in the same fashion.*

Second, Scripture plainly acknowledges the concept of tradition and recognizes as an inevitability that as humans pass things on to one another, some form of tradition is going to exist. For example, Paul speaks of having "passed on" the gospel (1 Corinthians 15:3 NIV), using a verb directly related to the activity of delivering a tradition. However, what is equally clear (though normally ignored by those who promote a form of Scripture + tradition = ultimate authority) is that all forms of

[4]Or rival. See chapter 9.

tradition, even those that claim divine origin and sanction, are to be subjected to the higher authority of the enscripturated Word. Jesus taught that even those traditions the Jews believed came from Moses were to be subjected to correction by Scripture (Matthew 15:1–9; Mark 7:5–13). When Paul tells the Thessalonians to hold to the "traditions" they were taught by word or by letter, it's obvious in context that he is referring to the gospel itself,[5] which had been both preached to them (when Paul was with them) and written to them (in his first epistle). Tradition is never said to be "God-breathed"[6] and is never exalted to a place of equality with (or supremacy over) the Scriptures.

ARGUMENT THREE

I still own the small brown-leather, red-lettered King James Bible my parents gave me on my seventh birthday. I remember proudly taking it to church the next Sunday; unlike the one I had before, with a zipper and pictures on the cover, this one looked like an adult's Bible. How serious I must have seemed that day in Sunday school.

I am so thankful for all my Sunday school teachers, beginning with my mother. We didn't just sit around and entertain ourselves—we really learned the Word, including the Old Testament (which doesn't happen so often today). Somewhere along the road I learned the following verse:

> Thy word have I hid in mine heart, that I might not sin against thee. (Psalm 119:11)

Around the time I received my new Bible, I was sent to the principal's office at school for the first time. You see, I was passing out tracts on the playground and talking about Christ to my schoolmates, and my teacher didn't like it; even back in the late 1960s the degradation of the educational system that has led to the modern American anti-Christian stance had begun. I walked into the principal's office and, somewhat to my own

---

[5] 2 Thessalonians 2:15 will be treated more fully in chapter 9.
[6] Cf. 2 Timothy 3:16–17.

surprise, handed him a tract. (He looked a bit taken aback as well, perhaps a portent of things to come). After reading it, he instructed me that while I could hand out tracts and talk to my classmates about what they said, I couldn't force anyone to take them. I found this rather strange—until the eighth grade I was rather small, so my young mind had difficulty grasping the idea of forcing anyone to take a tract.

A few years later my mother took me to her place of employment, a printing facility. I do not remember how it began, but I found myself standing before ink-soiled men twice my size, attempting to defend my faith. I doubt I made much of an impression with my arguments, but I remember clearly being challenged and amazed at the disbelief expressed by these hardened men. How could anyone not believe in God? How could anyone dispute His Word?

During my sophomore year of high school I came to understand the importance of divine truths, verities that last forever. I committed myself to reading through the Bible in a year after reading a Jack Chick comic about how embarrassing it would be to run into Habakkuk in heaven when you hadn't read his book while on earth. (I still remember reading the prophet's book that night and resting a little easier knowing that I now didn't have to be concerned about such an encounter.)

After I began earning money, I went to the local Christian bookstore and bought a Bible that is still one of my favorites: a *New Scofield Reference Bible,* Oxford edition. God blessed the cow that donated its cover; I had never felt leather so soft, so supple, or so smooth. I began devouring it, marking verses all through Romans and Galatians and John. The grandness of God's divine plan, the scope of the gospel, the glory of the Atonement began to come into focus. And my love of the Bible as God's Word became overpowering.

It was at this time that I experienced an intense, deeply rooted desire to memorize the Scriptures. This longing did not arise from some challenge or some apologetic encounter. I do not recall it coming from a sermon, a Bible study, or a discussion with a fellow believer. As I was reading God's living words there was an almost insatiable passion to make them a part of my innermost being. I was not satisfied to have these precious words external to me, in a book—I wanted them within me, wherever I went. And so I began. One of my strongest spiritual impressions comes from a summer day, home alone, spent walking up and down the one hallway in our house, repeatedly repeating John 1:1–18 until I had it memorized. The contemplation of the eternality of the Word, and the wonder of the Word becoming flesh, was magnified and burned into my soul through the memorization of God's words.

Another strong memory from that same summer involved memorizing Psalm 1 and feeling so close to the psalmist who wrote,

> Blessed is the man that walketh not in the counsel of the ungodly, nor standeth in the way of sinners, nor sitteth in the seat of the scornful. But his delight is in the law of the LORD; and in his law doth he meditate day and night. (vv. 1–2)

How could I meditate upon the law of the Lord day and night if that Word was not *within me, part of me?* As a young person, entering into adulthood and preparing to make major decisions about the rest of my life, choosing to set God's law as the focus of my attention and the center of my life and thought was absolutely essential.

––––––

A quarter of a century later I still love the Word of God. As with a thriving marriage, that love has grown more mature, rooted in much more knowledge but no less passionate. That original longing for the Word has proven to be supernatural in origin, for it did not pass with the changing of the years, marriage, children, or career. It abides with me always, guides and directs my decisions, oversees my life. My Savior has spoken through His Word, and His Spirit continually drives me to it as my foundation of truth and wisdom.

THREE ARGUMENTS EVALUATED

You've probably noted the stark contrast between the preceding three sections. And if you're a child of the postmodern period, influenced as we all are by the sound-bite world around us, you found each progressive argument a little easier to read and follow.

Specifically, the first argument is rather cold and analytical, based upon observations, logic, and unspoken philosophy. It speaks to a much smaller portion of our world today than it once did, but that doesn't mean it's unimportant, since many citizens of earth have decided, without once having directly considered it, that the argument presented here is completely without merit and utterly untenable. At times believers must dig down to this level to expose the faulty presuppositions that hold others back from seeing the truth.

The second argument is a little more familiar and friendly in that it's mainly biblical in nature. This is the argument we encounter when speaking with others who believe in some form of divine revelation (or at least the possibility thereof). Many of the world's religions promote a type or form of "scripture," and hence we recognize the need to be able to distinguish the Christian Scriptures from other writings regarded as holy. At the same time many "Christian" groups seek to add to the Scriptures some ultimate authority outside of God's words, and therefore we must diligently examine all such claims in defense of the truth.

My personal story (the third argument), true as it is, only speaks to one aspect of scriptural sufficiency. My testimony is one of countless thousands today and over the course of history. But it is just that, a personal testimony. It speaks to others who have experienced the same or similar things in their own lives. It evokes a sympathetic response in the hearts of fellow believers and, for that reason, is probably more memorable for most than the first two sections.

So why begin with these three brief arguments? To lay a foundation for what is to come. Each of these discussion-types goes into the full-orbed doctrine of *sola scriptura,* a belief not held in isolation but part of the fabric of Christian truth itself. Its foundations go deep into the very foundation of the faith, touching upon issues that do not often receive attention in today's churches. Cut off those foundations, and the belief is open to attack and denial. Ignore those foundations and the relationship of this truth to the rest of Christian doctrine, and run the danger of creating a shallow imitation of the reality, a doctrine to be abandoned or compromised on a whim.

This divine truth is eminently logical and rational, *given a particular starting place*. This doctrine is consistent with biblical revelation, *given the proper application of sound exegetical rules*. And this doctrine is satisfying to human souls *given that the divine work of regeneration has taken place*. It is philosophically sound, biblically necessitated, and spiritually appraised and confirmed. So why doesn't everyone believe it?

Sola scriptura, like all divine truths, leads us to recognize God's awesome glory and our desperate need. Just as for salvation we are completely dependent upon the all-sufficient grace of God, so too we are dependent upon His self-revelation for knowledge of our Savior, His work, the gospel, and everything else contained in divine revelation. To believe in *sola scriptura* is to allow God to speak without interruption. It is to trust His self-revelation, refusing to mix man's words with God's, man's thoughts with His thoughts. It is to be quiet and to let God speak. Consistently believing and practicing *sola scriptura* requires a deep-seated commitment that comes to the human heart solely through the work of the Holy Spirit in bringing spiritual life.

This explains, then, why every attack upon the Christian faith includes, in some form or another, a denial of *sola scriptura*. Whether it takes the form of blatant denial of scriptural inspiration or comes in the subtle assertion of the need for an "infallible authority" to interpret the Bible for you, the goal is the same. God's voice is either completely muted or blended in with the voice of man so that one is never sure which voice is speaking. In either case, the authority of God's Word is compromised and room is made for man's ideas and schemes.

This is why the doctrine of *sola scriptura* is denied on every hand today. Just as man's pride wishes to insert human actions and merit into the gospel, so that we can boast, at least a bit, in our own accomplishments (thus denying the sufficiency of God's grace), so too man seeks to enthrone his own thoughts and authority in place of the ultimate authority of God's Word so as to allow man to control God's truth. This is the basis of every false teaching, every error the church has ever faced or ever will face.

CHAPTER 2

Definitions:
More Than Half
the Battle

After engaging hundreds, possibly thousands of individuals over the sufficiency of Scripture, I have come to realize that 85 percent of the battle is fought over definitions. Few of the arguments against biblical sufficiency in matters of faith and morals are truly compelling *if* one is fully aware of the real issues. In fact, many who have abandoned their faith in this doctrine have done so not because the arguments against it were overwhelming but because they held to a flawed, incomplete, and simply erroneous concept to begin with. Straw men have never been known to put up much of a fight, hence, trying to defend an errant view of *sola scriptura* always results in defeat.

Sola scriptura literally means "Scripture alone." Unfortunately, this phrase tends to be taken in the vein of "Scripture in isolation, Scripture outside of the rest of God's work in the church."[1] That is *not* its intended meaning; again, it means "Scripture alone as the sole infallible rule of faith for the

---

[1] See also chapter 9 for further treatment.

church." As mentioned previously, it is a positive assertion of
the nature and traits of Scripture as well as a negative statement
indicating that only Scripture possesses its unique capacities as
the rule of faith. *A rule of faith is that which governs and guides
what we believe and why.* One work, placing the phrase in its historical setting (the Reformation), defines *sola scriptura* as "the
freedom of Scripture to rule as God's word in the church, dis-
entangled from papal and ecclesiastical magisterium and tradition."[2]

The reason men's religions must deny this truth is simple,
for the corollary of *sola scriptura* is that *all a person must believe to
be a follower of Christ is found in Scripture and in no other source.* If
it has been given to us in Scripture by the Holy Spirit, then it is
binding upon the believer's heart and conscience. We cannot
pick and choose what we will and will not believe: If it is the
infallible rule of faith, it must be believed.[3] Here is how I
expressed it when defending this belief in a public debate a
number of years ago:

> The Bible claims to be the *sole and sufficient* infallible
> rule of faith for the Christian church. The Scriptures are
> not in need of any supplement; their authority comes
> from their nature as God-breathed revelation; their
> authority is *not* dependent upon man, church, or council.
> The Scriptures are self-consistent, self-interpreting, and
> self-authenticating. The Christian church looks to the
> Scriptures as the only infallible and sufficient rule of faith,
> and the church is always subject to the Word, and is con-
> stantly reformed thereby.

I am an elder in a Reformed Baptist church;[4] we use, *as a*

---

[2]David F. Wright, "Protestantism" in *Evangelical Dictionary of Theology,* ed., Walter A. Elwell (Baker, 1984), 889.

[3]This does not mean we must have an infallible knowledge of Scripture, for no one (except the Lord Jesus Christ) has ever had such a knowledge. The point is, if we know something is revealed in Scripture, we must believe it. We cannot reject what we know to be a scriptural truth and at the same time claim to be a Christian. And the "nonne-gotiables," those things that define the faith, will be found *only* in Scripture. To reject them is to reject the faith itself.

[4]Since Reformed Baptists are not the largest group on the planet, I often get a look of confusion when I use the term. For those interested in knowing more about the dis-tinctives, we have placed an article on our particular (local body) Web site (*www.prbc.org*) titled "What Is a Reformed Baptist Church?" Also available is a sermon I presented, "Why I Am a Reformed Baptist."

subordinate standard,[5] the London Baptist Confession of 1689 as a sufficient statement of the faith of our church. In most matters the LBC of 1689 is word-for-word identical to the great Westminster Confession of 1648 and, with only a few exceptions, is identical in the following citations, indicating the unanimity on the nature of Scripture expressed here between Baptists and Presbyterians.

> The authority of the Holy Scripture, for which it ought to be believed, and obeyed, dependeth not upon the testimony of any man, or Church; but wholly upon God (who is truth itself) the author thereof: and therefore it is to be received, because it is the Word of God. (1:4)

Many of the dialogues in *Scripture Alone* will develop this section's assertion—based upon the teachings of Matthew 22:31; 2 Timothy 3:14–17; and 2 Peter 1:20–21—that Scripture's authority is inherent in its nature as the very speech of God. Given the ultimacy of the author, the Scriptures can boast of no higher authority attesting to their truth than that which they themselves give. This is a fact well known to generations past but often lost in our day. Keep this in mind—it will come up over and over again.

As I noted above, "Scripture alone" does not mean "Scripture isolated." The Word is divine, and the Spirit who gave it does not will to be separated from His masterpiece. Read these words from the Confession:

> We may be moved and induced by the testimony of the Church of God to an high and reverent esteem of the Holy Scripture, and the heavenliness of the matter, the efficacy of the doctrine, the majesty of the style, the consent of all the parts, the scope of the whole (which is to give all glory to God), the full discovery it makes of the only way of man's salvation, the many other incomparable excellencies, and the entire perfection thereof, are arguments whereby it doth abundantly evidence itself to be the Word of God; yet,

---

[5]Note the consistency: The confession is *subordinate* to the *ultimate* authority of Scripture. It is a statement of faith, an explanation of what we believe; its authority, as all ecclesiastical authorities must, bows to Scripture's authority.

notwithstanding, our full persuasion and assurance of the infallible truth, and divine authority thereof, is from the inward work of the Holy Spirit bearing witness by and with the word in our hearts. (1:5)

Many of the dialogues in this book will end with the recognition that outside of the Holy Spirit's work in man's heart and mind, even the plainest truths, which seem so utterly compelling to the renewed mind and the regenerated heart, remain "foolishness" and a "stumbling block" (1 Corinthians 1:18ff.) [6]

We then come to the specific delineation of the doctrine of *sola scriptura*. The LBC begins with these words:

The Holy Scripture is the only sufficient, certain, and infallible rule of all saving knowledge, faith, and obedience, although the light of nature, and the works of creation and providence do so far manifest the goodness, wisdom, and power of God, as to leave men inexcusable; yet are they not sufficient to give that knowledge of God and his will which is necessary unto salvation. Therefore it pleased the Lord at sundry times and in divers manners to reveal himself, and to declare that his will unto his church; and afterward for the better preserving and propagating of the truth, and for the more sure establishment and comfort of the church against the corruption of the flesh, and the malice of Satan, and of the world, to commit the same wholly unto writing; which maketh the Holy Scriptures to be most necessary, those former ways of God's revealing his will unto his people being now ceased. (1:1)

These words were chosen carefully, so note them well. *Sufficient, certain,* and *infallible.* Three attributes of divine Scripture that nothing else can begin to approach. Test any pretended contender for the throne of the church's allegiance, and you will find it isn't sufficient in its scope and matter, certain in its

---

[6]Many a believer, not recognizing the absolute necessity of the Spirit's work in freeing a person from slavery to sin, experiences great frustration when presenting (to an unbeliever) truths that seem so self-evident to those of the faith. Yes, there are compelling factual arguments that point to the nature and sufficiency of Scripture, but the mind darkened in sin will refuse to see and acknowledge those arguments. Indeed, even as believers we are utterly dependent upon the work of the Spirit to enlighten our minds and give us understanding.

nature and content, or infallible in its consistency and authority.

The confession recognizes the existence of "general revelation," the revelation given in nature whereby God shows Himself to be the all-powerful Creator, rendering humans accountable to honor Him as God and give thanks to Him (Romans 1:20–21). Even so, the LBC rightfully says that general revelation is insufficient to communicate the gospel itself. Instead, God has chosen to commit His truth to writing. Why? For the "better preserving and propagating of the truth and for the more sure establishment and comfort of the church." These truths will also regularly reappear in the dialogues that follow.

> The whole counsel of God, concerning all things necessary for His own glory, man's salvation, faith and life, is either expressly set down or necessarily contained in the Holy Scripture: unto which nothing at any time is to be added, whether by new revelations of the Spirit, or traditions of men. Nevertheless, we acknowledge the inward illumination of the Spirit of God to be necessary for the saving understanding of such things as are revealed in the word; and that there are some circumstances concerning the worship of God, and government of the Church, common to human actions and societies, which are to be ordered by the light of nature, and Christian prudence, according to the general rules of the word, which are always to be observed. (1:6)
>
> All things in Scripture are not alike plain in themselves, nor alike clear unto all; yet those things which are necessary to be known, believed, and observed for salvation, are so clearly propounded, and opened in some place of Scripture or other, that not only the learned, but the unlearned, in a due use of the ordinary means, may attain unto a sufficient understanding of them. (1:7)

Here is where the reality of *sola scriptura* comes to expression. What is the Scripture sufficient to reveal with clarity? "All things necessary for [God's] own glory, man's salvation, faith and life." In Scripture, these things are either revealed "expressly" or are "necessarily contained." That is, we are not limited only to the words of Scripture, but we must also believe what the Scriptures lead us to believe through the entire spectrum of their teaching. The most obvious example of this is the divine doctrine of the Trinity: while the term itself (*Trinity*) is not found in the Bible, the doctrines that not only lead us to it but in fact *demand* we believe it (monotheism, the equality of the divine persons, the distinction of the divine persons) are plainly stated in Scripture, thus the doctrine is *necessarily* contained in the words God used to teach it.

Obviously, this is not a claim that the Bible is the complete storehouse of all knowledge, divine and human. It is manifestly limited from the divine side, for as we are told in Deuteronomy 29:29, "The secret things belong to the LORD our God." The Bible does not exhaust the truth about God—indeed, even eternity itself will not accomplish this. The same is true about human knowledge. The Bible does not tell you everything you need to know to perform brain surgery or to figure out your tax forms. God's Word is not intended to inform you on the formation of tidewater glaciers or to give you exhaustive instructions on the use of a centrifuge in biochemical analysis. Arguments that prove the Bible cannot do these things are not arguments against *sola scriptura;* what Scripture *is* sufficient for must be kept clearly in mind.

The LBC likewise addresses (in 1:6–7) another vital aspect of the truth: the Bible is not a simplistic user's manual. It isn't arranged with a "Quick Start" section for those in a hurry. It doesn't have topical and subject indexes, and some parts are more difficult to understand than others. Instead, "those things which are necessary to be known, believed, and observed for salvation" are to be found in Scripture so that not only the learned but also the unlearned may, "in a due use of the ordinary means," come to a sufficient understanding. This too will come out in the discussions that follow.

So to summarize, the Scriptures are the sole sufficient, certain, infallible rule of faith for the church—they alone reveal all that is necessary to be believed for salvation and a godly life. But we might clarify this definition even more by noting some of the most common misrepresentations of *sola scriptura.*

WHAT SOLA SCRIPTURA IS *NOT*

The following dialogue between Joshua, our defender of *sola scriptura*, and Robert, a Roman Catholic, closely parallels the persistent arguments of today's Catholic apologists. Many are likewise used by other groups.

JOSHUA: So we see that Paul directed Timothy to the Scriptures *alone* as the source of his ability to do everything God called him to do in the church.[7]

ROBERT: But *sola scriptura* is clearly unscriptural, a manmade tradition. Think about it: The Bible does not tell us all sorts of things. How can you say it is *sufficient?*

JOSHUA: As I just noted, Timothy was equipped by the Scriptures to do his work in the church. I never said the Bible could have told him everything he needed to know about being a goldsmith or a tentmaker or a sailor. The Bible surely speaks to all of human endeavor in that we are to do all things to the glory of God, but I never claimed it tells us everything there is to know. You do not understand the doctrine if you think we claim the Bible is a repository of all knowledge, divine and human. It is the *rule of faith,* not the Universal Encyclopedia.

ROBERT: Joshua, the Bible actually *denies* that it is the complete rule of faith. John tells us that not everything concerning Christ's work is in Scripture:[8]

> And there are also many other things which Jesus did, which if they were written in detail, I suppose that even the world itself would not contain the books which were written.[9]

JOSHUA: Again, Robert, this shows a fundamental misunderstanding of the doctrine you are denying. Yes, many of Jesus' words and actions are not recorded in Scripture— they weren't intended to be. It is not necessary that the Bible contain every single possible detail about the life and ministry of Jesus for it to function just as God intended, as

---

[7]See 2 Timothy 3.
[8]These are the direct words of Roman Catholic apologist Karl Keating in *Catholicism and Fundamentalism* (Ignatius Press, 1988), 136.
[9]John 21:25.

the sole infallible rule of faith for the church.

Think about it: Do you need to know the style and color of the robe Peter was wearing on the Mount of Transfiguration? The weight and birth date of the donkey upon which Jesus rode into Jerusalem, or the genus and species of the palm branches laid before Him? And if you think your "tradition" fills in all these blanks, can you point me to where Rome has answered these very questions, or has infallibly defined even a single word spoken by the Lord Jesus or any of the apostles that is *not* contained in Scripture?[10]

ROBERT: Well, I don't know of any, but you have to admit that *sola scriptura* is completely unworkable, a blueprint for anarchy! Look at what it's done to the Protestant church. I've heard there are more than 28,000 Protestant denominations because of *sola scriptura*, with more springing up every day. Surely that's not what God intended—He wants us to be one, as Jesus says in John 17.

JOSHUA: Ah, two common errors rolled into a single argument! Let's dismiss the 28,000-denominations argument right off the bat. Dr. Eric Svendsen has expertly documented[11] that this number is grossly inflated, and if you actually traced back to the sources, you'd discover that if you held yourself to the same standards, Roman Catholicism would represent literally hundreds of denominations itself. Do you buy that?

ROBERT: I haven't looked at that, but no, there is only one church.

JOSHUA: I'd recommend a look at the actual data.[12] Despite the popularity of the 28,000-denominations claim, it holds no water. But beyond this, asserting that *sola scriptura* is to blame for fundamental disagreements shows an even deeper misunderstanding of the issues. I would like to think

[10]This section of the dialogue reflects the interchange between myself and Fr. Mitchell Pacwa in a debate held in December of 1999 in San Diego. When I asked him specifically if the Roman Church had ever infallibly defined a single word uttered by the Lord Jesus or the apostles that is not contained in Scripture, he frankly admitted that no such definition has ever been offered.
[11]Eric Svendsen, *Upon This Slippery Rock* (Calvary Press, 2002), 58–64.
[12]Ibid.

the majority of those who promote such an argument have simply not thought through what they are saying. Let me ask you: Are there disagreements among Roman Catholics as to theological beliefs? Differences of view on the nature of tradition, or on what amounts to an infallible pronouncement, or on other similar matters?

ROBERT: Well, you know the answer to that question, Joshua, but I point out that those are not central issues.

JOSHUA: The nature of tradition is certainly important, but even granting your objection, I would point out that the depth of agreement between groups who accept the Bible alone without any external "infallible" authorities and interpreters on the central issues[13] is great indeed. You would agree, then, that despite the existence of the magisterial teaching of Rome, disagreements remain between Roman Catholics?

ROBERT: To some degree, yes.

JOSHUA: So is it not somewhat inconsistent to maintain that for Protestants the Bible has to produce perfect unanimity of opinion when the addition of Rome's teaching authority has not accomplished the same thing for Catholics?

ROBERT: But if it is truly sufficient . . .

JOSHUA: . . . to do what God intends it to do, yes, but why do you assume that for *sola scriptura* to be correct, God had to have intended us to have perfect unanimity of opinion?

ROBERT: Jesus said we would all be one, did He not?

JOSHUA: Yes, as Jesus indicates, we are to be one in Him and in the Father,[14] but you are going way too far to assume that this precludes differences of viewpoint, let alone false teachers or heretics. In fact, Paul told the Ephesian elders before he left them that men would arise from their own ranks and lead the sheep astray.[15] In similar fashion, he told Timothy

---

[13]Such as monotheism, the deity and centrality of Christ, the deity of the Holy Spirit, supernaturalism, creation, revelation, the judgment of God, the need for redemption, the resurrection, etc.

[14]See John 17.

[15]Recorded in Acts 20:29–31.

that deceivers would grow worse and worse.[16] Please note, Robert, that in both instances Paul's solution was *not* to direct anyone to the bishop of Rome or any such authority. Each time Paul directed those he had warned concerning false teachers to *look to the Word of God.*

I want to emphasize something else, too. Have you ever changed printers on your computer system?

ROBERT: Yes, just recently, in fact. The never-ending cycle of upgrade, upgrade, upgrade.

JOSHUA: I know it well. When you did so, did you do what most men do and just plug the thing in to see if it would work, or did you read the instructions first?

ROBERT: Well, it says, "Plug and play."

JOSHUA: Yes. And if it had gone wrong, would you have blamed the instructions you didn't read?

ROBERT: I think I have done that, actually, but of course I realize there's no basis for blaming unread instructions.

JOSHUA: Exactly. And let me ask something else: Did you sort of assume that your new printer would work the same way as your old one, but then need to be adjusted when it worked a little differently?

ROBERT: Sure did. But I don't get where you're headed.

JOSHUA: Well, it's like this: Just as it's not the instructions' fault if you have problems with your printer, so it's not the Bible's fault if people don't read it. Coming to the Scriptures with our traditions is like carrying over "traditions" from your old printer. Is it the instructions' fault that you assumed the printer would work in a way it didn't? Or, what if you picked which sections of the instruction manual you wanted to read and which you didn't, just as people pick and choose which passages of Scripture they will or will not heed? You can have the perfect instruction manual, clear, perspicuous—might I say infallible?—but this will not, by itself, guarantee that you will use the printer perfectly, does it?

---

[16] 2 Timothy 3:13.

ROBERT: But the Lord said we should be one; so if His Word is all we have—

JOSHUA: I didn't say it's "all we have." I said it is the sole infallible rule of faith. I never said it exists in a vacuum; I never said the community of faith is devoid of the Spirit; I never said that elders have no authority, etc. The point of the illustration is that blaming the Scriptures for what people do with them is an approach that should be rejected, and indeed ridiculed, by any serious-minded individual.

ROBERT: But *sola scriptura* does lead to an extreme form of individualism! You can't have an authoritative church and *sola scriptura* at the same time.

JOSHUA: Why should we buy into the "you and your Bible under a tree in the woods alone" *or* "the infallible Pope in Rome" false dichotomy? I think most folks can see a pretty wide spectrum of belief that exists between the two extremes. What if the Bible, read in its own context and allowed to speak with the authority of divine revelation, teaches us that Christ has established His church and organized it in such a way as to provide His people with godly men entrusted with the duty to teach and preach and shepherd and guide, all *under* the ultimate authority of Christ, manifested by His Spirit and the Word? Could the Scriptures do that?

ROBERT: Of course, but how can that really work when *sola scriptura* denies authority to anything but a Bible that, in the final analysis, must be interpreted by each individual?

JOSHUA: *Balance* is the key in many areas of the Christian life. Rome's claim to ultimacy in doctrinal and spiritual matters lacks balance, just as the "lone-ranger Christian" viewpoint lacks balance. The Bible, being God-breathed, partakes of the very authority of God Himself. As such, it cannot possibly embrace a *non-divine* authority alongside itself. However, this does not for a moment mean that God cannot set up subordinate authorities that are vitally important and necessary for the proper health and balance of the believing community and the individual believer—authorities that look to and draw from that divine authority while never eclipsing it or replacing it.

ROBERT: But I've talked to many Protestants who find the constant difficulties they face in the church, especially over personal disputes and doctrinal divisions, to be a great hindrance and cause of despair.

JOSHUA: So have I. My heart grieves over schisms and controversies and all the other assorted problematic issues in the church. Paul's heart broke over the same issues! If such difficulties existed when apostles chosen directly by the Lord Jesus Christ, through whom revelation came and Scripture was written, walked the earth and ministered in the churches, then upon what logical basis are we to believe that it is God's intention to banish such troubles from the church *after* the apostolic age? Will not the church always struggle against false sons in her midst, against wolves in sheep's clothing? If the existence of such difficulties indicates a problem with *sola scriptura*, then would it not follow that there was something "wrong" or "insufficient" in the apostolic ministry of Paul or Peter or John as well?

ROBERT: An interesting point, Joshua, but one of the problems I've always had with *sola scriptura* is that there was obviously a point in time when it simply could not have been true. What I mean is, there was a time when God's Word was communicated orally—for example, in the preaching and teaching of the apostles or in the ministry of the prophets. If *sola scriptura* could not have been true at that time, how can it be true now?

JOSHUA: Your question contains its own answer, Robert, for we both acknowledge that something was going on *then* that is not going on *now*. Rome agrees that the special activity of revealing Scripture ended with the apostolic era, and that the church's role is one of communicating an already given body of truth, not of producing "new revelation." So you do confess that something was true then that is not true today. Something has changed. We both agree that God has given us inspired revelation that He has spoken. The question is, how do we recognize that revelation today? Is it clear and easily distinguished or is it in some sense "secret" and known only to a particular group of leaders?

ROBERT: So you're saying that *sola scriptura* is only true at times?

JOSHUA: The question *sola scriptura* addresses is, "In the normal existence of the church down through the ages, what is God's intended means of conveying His truth to His church?" God did not continue the ministry of apostles down through the ages,[17] so what rule of faith has He given us by which we can maintain the purity of the gospel? Has He given us a Scripture that is subject to a higher authority and a body of unwritten, oral traditions, which content we can only know when its guardians choose to reveal small portions thereof?

Returning to your question, *sola scriptura* can be true when the *scriptura* exists in such a form as to be able to function as the rule of faith. Logically, during times of revelation, what was possessed by the church as God-breathed revelation was in transition. When that process came to an end (enscripturation), what was and is the final authority? That which is produced by the Spirit (Scripture), or that which is claimed by an ecclesiastical group as "tradition" but which we cannot test or observe over time?

ROBERT: You don't seem to like the word *tradition*.

JOSHUA: Well, you must confess it repeatedly appears in the Scriptures in a negative light. I am well aware that "tradition" can have a positive meaning, and believe me, I know that everyone, including myself, has "traditions."

---

[17]Latter-day Saints disagree, claiming their prophets and apostles do, in fact, continue just such a ministry. Though a refutation of this claim is beyond the scope of this work (see my *Letters to a Mormon Elder* [Bethany House, 1993], and Richard Abanes, *One Nation Under Gods* [Four Walls Eight Windows, 2002], for relevant discussions), the New Testament evidence is decidedly against such a concept. This evidence points to the cessation of the particular, distinguishable apostolic ministry, including the identification of only twelve apostles as late as the book of Revelation (21:14), the qualifications of that special apostleship precluding its continuation past the early decades of the church, and the form of the church as described in the pastoral epistles, where elders and deacons are the normative church offices, with no mechanisms put in place for the continuance of any other church office.

ROBERT: The difference is between godly traditions and human traditions.

JOSHUA: I would agree only if you mean "godly" in the sense of *those traditions which are subordinate to Scripture, corrected by Scripture, and lead to further godliness through order in worship and the promotion of true piety.* All such traditions are human, in the sense that they are not God-breathed. The key fact with tradition is that all traditions, even those that men claim have come from God, are to be tested by the higher authority of Scripture.[18] So the real issue is, does your tradition bow in submission to Scripture, or does your tradition force Scripture into subservience?

ROBERT: What makes tradition different is that we have the living voice of the Spirit in the Church.

JOSHUA: The role of the Spirit is unquestionably vital in the church. Everyone agrees on that point.

ROBERT: But doesn't *sola scriptura* in essence "muzzle the Spirit"?

JOSHUA: Some believe so, but that would also require us to believe the Spirit cannot give a living, scriptural revelation that speaks to every generation. We know that the Scriptures are the delight of the spiritually minded man, and that he meditates upon them day and night.[19] Believing in *sola scriptura* only means that God has chosen the *means* by which He will guide His people for His own honor and glory. The intimate relationship between the Word and the Spirit, found throughout Scripture, neither necessitates an "open canon," so that further revelation can be added, nor requires us to believe in some other "source" or "form" of revelation or the need of a human authority to "fill in" where Scripture falls short. The Spirit "birthed" the Scriptures; hence, there cannot possibly be any contradiction or disharmony between His leading and the Scriptures themselves.

---

[18]See Matthew 15:1–9; Mark 7:5–13.
[19]See Psalm 1.

After having a conversation like this, Joshua and Robert would have a significantly better chance of meaningfully discussing *sola scriptura* than takes place in most apologetic conversations today. Definitions must be established so that real *communication* can take place. Often, merely clearing up misconceptions can open wide the door to positive proclamation of God's truth.

THE CAMBRIDGE DECLARATION

In April of 1996 the Alliance of Confessing Evangelicals produced what has become known as The Cambridge Declaration. With almost prophetic foresight, this document speaks directly to the issues that sadly have only increased in their magnitude and in the danger they pose to Christ's church. Since *Scripture Alone* firmly embraces the vital importance of *sola scriptura* as a foundational truth, these words from the declaration's prologue provide external verification of the importance of our theme:

> Today the light of the Reformation has been significantly dimmed. The consequence is that the word "evangelical" has become so inclusive as to have lost its meaning. We face the peril of losing the unity it has taken centuries to achieve. Because of this crisis and because of our love of Christ, his gospel and his church, we endeavor to assert anew our commitment to the central truths of the Reformation and of historic evangelicalism. These truths we affirm not because of their role in our traditions, but because we believe that they are central to the Bible.

Sola Scriptura: The Erosion of Authority

> Scripture alone is the inerrant rule of the church's life, but the evangelical church today has separated Scripture from its authoritative function. In practice, the church is guided, far too often, by the culture. Therapeutic technique, marketing strategies, and the beat of the entertainment world often have far more to say about what the

church wants, how it functions and what it offers, than does the Word of God. Pastors have neglected their rightful oversight of worship, including the doctrinal content of the music. As biblical authority has been abandoned in practice, as its truths have faded from Christian consciousness, and as its doctrines have lost their saliency, the church has been increasingly emptied of its integrity, moral authority and direction.

Rather than adapting Christian faith to satisfy the felt needs of consumers, we must proclaim the law as the only measure of true righteousness and the gospel as the only announcement of saving truth. Biblical truth is indispensable to the church's understanding, nurture and discipline.

Scripture must take us beyond our perceived needs to our real needs and liberate us from seeing ourselves through the seductive images, clichés, promises, and priorities of mass culture. It is only in the light of God's truth that we understand ourselves aright and see God's provision for our need. The Bible, therefore, must be taught and preached in the church. Sermons must be expositions of the Bible and its teachings, not expressions of the preachers' opinions or the ideas of the age. We must settle for nothing less than what God has given.

The work of the Holy Spirit in personal experience cannot be disengaged from Scripture. The Spirit does not speak in ways that are independent of Scripture. Apart from Scripture we would never have known of God's grace in Christ. The biblical Word, rather than spiritual experience, is the test of truth.

Thesis One: Sola Scriptura

We reaffirm the inerrant Scripture to be the sole source of written divine revelation, which alone can bind the conscience. The Bible alone teaches all that is necessary for our salvation from sin and is the standard by which all Christian behavior must be measured. We deny that any creed, council or individual may bind a Christian's conscience, that the Holy Spirit speaks independently of or contrary to what is set forth in the Bible, or that personal spiritual experience can ever be a vehicle of revelation.

CHAPTER 3

Forever Settled: The Nature of God's Holy Word

Forever, O LORD, Your word is settled in heaven. (Psalm 119:89)

How one views Scripture will determine the rest of one's theology. There is no more basic issue: Every system of thought that takes seriously the claims of the Bible to be the inspired, authoritative Word of God will share a commitment to particular central truths, and that without compromise. Those systems that do not begin with this belief in Scripture will exhibit a wide range of beliefs that will shift over time in light of the ever-changing whims and views of culture. Almost every single collapse involving denominations and churches in regard to historic Christian beliefs can be traced back to a degradation in that group's view of the Bible as the inspired and inerrant revelation of God's truth. Once this foundation is lost, the house that was built upon it cannot long stand.

There is little worth in speaking of the sufficiency of a non-inspired, errant collection of ancient works, which is why the denial of the inspired *nature* of Scripture inevitably leads to a denial of its ability to function as the sole infallible rule of faith for the church. Those who place the Bible upon the same plane as any other human production, even while granting it some level of historic or religious importance, cannot help but look for new sources of authority in "tradition" or "new revelation." *Sola scriptura* assumes that the *scriptura* is divine in nature; if it is not, then *sola scriptura* is meaningless. This is why so many formerly conservative groups—churches that once stood solidly in defense of scriptural integrity, the supernatural nature of the Christian faith, and the historic, fundamental doctrines that define Christianity today—embrace so many elements of a non-Christian worldview. At some point in their history the ability of Scripture to communicate truth with clarity and force was first compromised, then functionally denied. It may have been a long process. It may have included tremendous battles, with victories and defeats, gains and losses. There may have been church splits, even the formation of new denominations that could no longer in good conscience abide by the downgraded view of Scripture as it developed. But eventually the foundation was gone, the certainty of the message preached was lost, and the message itself was changed.

Almost every denial of biblical sufficiency finds its root in a misunderstanding of, or more likely, a direct rejection of, the true nature of Scripture. This likewise means the answers we need to provide to those who ask of us a reason for our acceptance of scriptural authority must start with a solid understanding of the nature of God's Word. Without that foundation, we run the risk of offering contradictory and refutable defenses of our faith's heart and soul.

So we begin with the key texts that lay out the nature of Scripture. The believer who masters these passages will have a solid foundation upon which to stand against the widest range of attacks upon biblical sufficiency.

BREATHED OUT BY GOD: PAUL'S TESTIMONY TO THE WORD (2 TIMOTHY 3:16–17)

This passage in 2 Timothy is so often discussed that sometimes we lose interest in it, thinking we've heard all there is to know. But Paul's words to Timothy, coming as they do in the last letter Paul writes to his dearly beloved son in the faith, should have the force of the final testament of a mighty man of God. Indeed, all of 2 Timothy (including its repeated exhortations to stand for sound doctrine) should be read in the light of Paul's impending departure from this world. The specter of death tends to focus one's thoughts upon what is truly important; Paul's urgent communication with Timothy should be allowed to speak today with the same fervor in which it was penned, for it contains the elements vital to the continuance of the church and the furtherance of the ministry.

The context of this passage is one of warning and commandment: warning of trying times ahead, commandment to hold fast to sound doctrine. This section of the letter begins, "But realize this, that in the last days difficult times will come" (3:1). The next twelve verses contain grave warnings about the trials and difficulties of the church and those men who would give their lives in her service and leadership. In regard to the list of sinful attitudes found in verses 2–4, it's easy for us to nod in agreement, thinking Paul is again talking about those outside the church, but he begins verse 5 by saying these traits (love of money, lack of love, lack of self-control, treachery, conceit, etc.) mark those who hold "to a form of godliness, although they have denied its power." These are men who claim to be Christians, the false brethren that Paul had struggled against his entire ministry (cf. Galatians 2:4–5; 2 Corinthians 11:26). He tells Timothy to "avoid such men as these," something he would not have to say if these people were outside the church; however, just as Paul had warned in Acts 20:30, these men arise from *within* the church. Difficult times will come indeed!

These false teachers among the people (cf. 2 Peter 2:1) enter into households taking people captive, and though they teach and teach and teach, those who listen never come to a knowledge of the truth, for their leaders are actually opposed to the truth (all the while claiming to be its servants). These men are not just confused about the truth, *they stand in opposition to it.* Paul saw the root of the problem: They were of a depraved mind and had been rejected from the faith. They clearly had once professed it, but they are *adokimos* (2 Timothy 3:8), a word referring to a failure of testing, hence, "worthless, disqualified." When their faithfulness to the truth was tested, they failed the examination. Paul knows such men will not make progress in the church, but they surely are able to make progress outside the church.

Upon delivery of this dire warning, Paul reminds Timothy that there is nothing new here. Paul had suffered persecution and had shown a Spirit-borne perseverance in the face of troubles, just as Timothy would have to in his own ministry; the Lord had rescued Paul, and he would rescue Timothy as well. Every generation of the church needs to be reminded that opposition is not something that should cause surprise, for "all who desire to live godly in Christ Jesus will be persecuted" (v. 12). How can Paul know that *all* who live godly in Christ Jesus will encounter this kind of hatred from the world? Because God has not chosen to remove false teachers from the experience of His church: "Evil men and impostors will proceed from bad to worse, deceiving and being deceived" (v. 13). These words plainly communicate evil motivations, for an "impostor" isn't who he is by chance or ignorance. These men actively seek to deceive, even in their self-deception.

Paul gives Timothy no indication that God will someday banish false teachers from disturbing the saints, at least not until that final day when the bride will be presented to her husband "having no spot or wrinkle" (Ephesians 5:27). So what is Timothy to do, now that Paul will no longer be there to give him guidance? If ever there was a point where the apostle would refer to some kind of extra-biblical source of sufficiency, it would be here. If Paul believed we should look to a papacy, or to some Spirit-led prophet, or to some group of leaders, or to some new source of revelation, this would be the place to delineate this all-important source of aid for his beloved Timothy. What he does instead is perfectly in line with the teaching of Moses, the prophets, the Psalter, and, most important, the Lord Jesus Christ: He directs Timothy to the God-breathed

Scriptures as the never-changing, always sufficient source of truth:

> You, however, continue in the things you have learned and become convinced of, knowing from whom you have learned them, and that from childhood you have known the sacred writings which are able to give you the wisdom that leads to salvation through faith which is in Christ Jesus. All Scripture is inspired by God and profitable for teaching, for reproof, for correction, for training in righteousness; so that the man of God may be adequate, equipped for every good work. (2 Timothy 3:14–17)

Contrasting him with evil men and impostors, Paul exhorts Timothy to remain true to God's truth, to continue in the things he has learned, not looking for something "new" to prop him up in his ministry. Timothy has learned and become convinced of the truth; he is standing in it now and is to persist therein. One of Timothy's considerations is to be the *source* of his learning: He learned the truth from trustworthy sources— from godly parents, especially—in his youth. Unlike the false teachers disqualified from the faith by their behavior, attitudes, and lack of godly character, Timothy could find a firm foundation, for those from whom he learned had proven themselves over time through godly character.

However, it was not simply learning the truth in his youth that alone provided his firm foundation; many people who learn in their youth are completely devoid of the most important elements of God's truth. From childhood, Timothy was blessed to have been instructed out of the "sacred writings," the Scriptures of the *Tanakh,* [1] the Old Covenant writings. Paul elsewhere describes the blessing of the Tanakh given to the Jews as the very "oracles of God" (Romans 3:2); Timothy has studied them, known them, from his youth. Unlike the flash-in-the-pan false teachers, the Scriptures had been his guide and his light throughout his life.

---

[1] *Tanakh,* a term referring to the TNK, the *Torah* (Law), the *Neviim* (Prophets), and the *Ketuvim* (Writings), a Jewish means of referring to what is commonly called the Old Testament.

Paul's next statement is difficult for many modern evangelicals to understand, for he says that those Scriptures "are able
to give you the wisdom that leads to salvation through faith
which is in Christ Jesus" (2 Timothy 3:15). The sacred writings
have a supernatural character: They have the ability to impart
wisdom, not just wisdom that allows a person to live life more
peacefully and successfully (though they surely can do that as
well), but spiritual wisdom that leads to salvation. This is consistent with the testimony of the Lord Himself after the Resurrection, when, walking with the two disciples on the road to
Emmaus, He opened the Scriptures up for them, and "beginning with Moses and with all the prophets, He explained to
them the things concerning Himself in all the Scriptures"
(Luke 24:27). The literal rendering of Paul's words (in 2 Timothy 3:15) is that the Scriptures are able to "make wise unto
salvation . . ." or "instruct unto salvation by faith in Christ
Jesus."

Even so, given the nature of the Tanakh, how can we say
that it can make one wise unto salvation through faith in
Christ? Surely we do not encounter in the Tanakh the kind of
clarity regarding the person and work of Christ and the gospel
message that we find in Romans, for example. But the message
of the apostles *is* based firmly in the Old Testament Scriptures,
in the messianic prophecies, in the pictures of Christ's work
through the sacrifices and offerings. It is Paul's position
throughout his teaching that the message of the gospel, including that salvation is by faith without works of human merit, is
not only *consistent* with the Old Testament revelation but is, in
fact, the natural, necessary *continuation* of it. Indeed, Paul had
earlier stood before King Agrippa and proclaimed,

> "And so, having obtained help from God, I stand to this
> day testifying both to small and great, stating nothing but
> what the Prophets and Moses said was going to take place;
> that the Christ was to suffer, and that by reason of His res-
> urrection from the dead He should be the first to proclaim
> light both to the Jewish people and to the Gentiles" (Acts
> 26:22–23).

Thus Paul's words to Timothy reflect a settled conclusion concerning the message of the old covenant Scriptures, a conclusion he certainly had communicated to his son in the faith at numerous times and in many ways.

And so it is the reference to Scripture and its role in salvation that prompts Paul to remind Timothy of their cherished common heritage. Note that *Paul is not announcing something new;* our frequent references to this passage might make it seem as if this is the only place where the Bible actually teaches its own inspired nature, but such would be to see the situation in reverse. *Paul is reminding Timothy of something old,* something basic, something foundational. This final epistle is filled not with new revelations but with exhortations to already established truths that Paul believes Timothy *must* understand and love and embrace. Timothy already knew of the divine nature of the Scriptures, but needed reminders, in the most sober of situations, of what God had provided for him as he faced many dangers and challenges.

THE TEACHING OF 2 TIMOTHY 3:16-17

All Scripture is inspired by God and profitable for teaching, for reproof, for correction, for training in righteousness; so that the man of God may be adequate, equipped for every good work.

The traditional translation of the first phrase is "All Scripture is inspired by God," but some modern translations have departed from this rendering. Note two especially:

All Scripture is breathed out by God and profitable for teaching, for reproof, for correction, and for training in righteousness, that the man of God may be competent, equipped for every good work. (ESV)

All Scripture is God-breathed and is useful for teaching, rebuking, correcting and training in righteousness, so that the man of God may be thoroughly equipped for every good work. (NIV)

These two contemporary renderings of the single Greek

term traditionally rendered "inspired," *theopneustos*, are "breathed out by God" and "God-breathed," respectively. Why such a major difference in translation? The modern translations are simply reflecting the validity of study done long ago by B. B. Warfield, the great Princeton theologian and scholar.[2] Upon completing an extensive examination of the uses, origin, derivation, and meaning of *theopneustos*, Warfield summarized:

> From all points of approach alike we appear to be conducted to the conclusion that [*theopneustos*] is primarily expressive of the origination of Scripture, not of its nature and much less of its effects. What is *theopneustos* is "God-breathed," produced by the creative breath of the Almighty. And Scripture is called *theopneustos* in order to designate it as "God-breathed," the product of Divine spiration, the creation of that Spirit who is in all spheres of the Divine activity the executive of the Godhead. The traditional translation of the word by the Latin *inspiratus a Deo* is no doubt also discredited, if we are to take it at the foot of the letter. It does not express a breathing *into* the Scriptures by God. . . . What it affirms is that the Scriptures owe their origin to an activity of God the Holy Ghost and are in the highest and truest sense His creation. It is on this foundation of Divine origin that all the high attributes of Scripture are built.[3]

It's hard to overemphasize the importance of understanding this: What Scripture is here teaching about itself, the term Paul uses, its consistency with the rest of biblical revelation, and comprehension of Warfield's explanation (above) may well be the most important exercise in developing a strong foundation in biblical sufficiency that gives rise to sound theology and apologetics. Warfield rightly concluded that the term translated "God-breathed" is speaking of the *origin* of the Scriptures; they

---

[2]Warfield's work on *theopneustos* first appeared in *The Presbyterian and Reformed Review* and is now reprinted in *The Inspiration and Authority of the Bible* (Presbyterian and Reformed, 1948), 245–96. Though in print for more than a century, and though great advances in the study of koine Greek have taken place since its publication, Warfield's conclusions have withstood both the passage of time and the critical examination of those who seek to establish a significantly less divine origin for the Christian Scriptures. Despite its complexity, the reader is directed to Warfield's work as an important element of study regarding this topic.

[3]Ibid., 296.

are not, first and foremost, in a primary sense, human in their origination, and we will see this truth repeated in different ways in other passages below. A solid view of the Bible begins with the recognition that God is its principle author, the origin and source of its very essence. All sub-Christian systems *must*, by definition, attack God's Word at this very point, for the survival of their unbiblical teachings and views of authority is dependent upon overthrowing this precise truth. Thus it is here that the battle is joined; we will continue to expand upon the importance of these facts as we examine the scriptural witness.

Having repeated the common Christian confession that Scripture has its origin in God and is divine in nature, Paul says (v. 16) that all Scripture is *"profitable* ("valuable," "useful," "beneficial") for *teaching"* (or "doctrine"); both terms[4] should be noted for their significance. The testimony of this passage is sometimes muted because people emphasize that something may be *profitable* without being *sufficient* for the task, as if Paul's point here is that Scripture, like so many other things, is "an assistant" to one who teaches, sort of like crayons and a flannel board might be "useful" in teaching Sunday school for six-year-olds. This is *not* the apostle's intention; Timothy didn't need teaching aids, but encouragement about what God has provided for him to fulfill the ministry he was given in light of Paul's soon departure.

The emphasis is upon "all," as in "all Scripture." *All* Scripture is God-breathed, and, because it is, *all* Scripture forms the basis, the foundation, upon which Timothy is to base his exhortation, his doctrine, his teaching. The true application of the text is not to open the door for other equally profitable things (Paul makes no reference to such sources for the man of God) but to extend the profitability of the Word across the entirety of God's work of inspiration: that is, *all* of the Scripture (yes, including the battles and the kings and the genealogical lists and the imprecatory psalms!) is profitable as sound doctrine and theology.

---

[4]Greek *ophelimos* and *didaskalian*, respectively.

The term translated "teaching" here is often translated "doctrine."[5] Paul uses it nineteen times in his epistles, and fifteen of those appearances are found in the pastoral epistles (1 and 2 Timothy, Titus), often in the context of an exhortation to stand for "sound, good, right, proper, honorable, fitting doctrine." When we recognize the interchangeability of "teaching" and "doctrine," the importance of the passage to the sufficiency of Scripture in matters of teaching and doctrine is more clearly seen. Paul knows Timothy must have an unswerving source; he had already exhorted him to seek "sound doctrine" (1 Timothy 1:10; cf. 4:6) and directly instructed him to pay close attention to preaching and to "doctrine" (or "teaching," 1 Timothy 4:13). How is Timothy to do this when Paul is gone? Not by relying upon emotions, for God has provided an unchanging basis for that "teaching" that is to be part and parcel of the public worship for Christ's church: the God-breathed Scriptures.

Commentators have noticed a relationship in the four primary terms Paul uses in this verse.[6] Some theorize a poetic relationship[7] here, with the first and fourth terms being in parallel to each other, leaving the second and third in the same relationship; that is, "for *doctrine/teaching*" is parallel to "for training/discipline in *righteousness*," and "for *reproof/rebuke*" is parallel to "for *correction*." This is possible, though one need not insist upon the parallelism. At any rate, it's useful to see the terms in these pairs, as this allows us to compare and contrast their meanings.

"For training in righteousness,"[8] the phrase related to "doctrine/teaching," is most expressive, referring to discipline and instruction, as one might provide to a child who is learning a skill or a sport. Paul may well be mirroring in these words to Timothy the vitally important truth contained in his reminder to Titus:

> For the grace of God has appeared, bringing salvation

---

[5]Ibid.
[6]Greek *didaskalian, elegmon, epanorthosin, dikaiosune.*
[7]A "chiasmic structure."
[8]Greek *paideian ten en dikaiosune.*

to all men, instructing us to deny ungodliness and worldly desires and to live sensibly, righteously and godly in the present age. (Titus 2:11–12)

Just as God's saving grace instructs those it saves, so too the Word of God trains, instructs, disciplines believers as they seek to live in the realm of righteousness. We are not accustomed to such living when we first come to Christ, of course, and hence must be instructed "in righteousness," which we can receive in the God-breathed Scriptures. The modern reader should pay close attention to what this means in our context: God's Word is able to provide us with the necessary foundation for sound ethical and moral action and thought. We can live in righteousness when we are willing to receive exhortation and instruction from Scripture; given the wholesale abandonment of the Bible as the source for our knowledge of how to live (accompanied by the rush to human philosophies and mechanisms), the professing church desperately needs these words to be heard once again.

Coming back to the "middle" primary terms Paul uses in verse 16,[9] their interplay, I believe, reflects the apostle's own experience in delivering God's truth to the church. "For *reproving/refuting*" can refer either to refuting false concepts/teachings or to rebuking sinful actions/attitudes. It probably carries both ideas, as both are the responsibilities of those who minister in the church. "For *reproving/refuting*" may be seen in Paul's use of a related term in Ephesians: "Do not participate in the unfruitful deeds of darkness, but instead even *expose [or rebuke]* them" (5:11).[10] "For *correction*" is found throughout Paul's letters, wherein he rebukes false living and false activity on the part of believers. In reality, there is no separating the two concepts,[11] as James made so clear.[12] Sound doctrine and sound living go hand in hand; an error in one normally leads to an error in the other, and Paul's speaking to the element of fault

---

[9]Greek *elegmon* and *epanorthosin*.
[10]Emphasis added. From Greek *elegcho*.
[11]"For reproving/refuting" and "for correction."
[12]In James 2:14–26. See my discussion of this important passage in *The God Who Justifies* (Bethany House, 2001), 329–54.

or error also speaks to the restoration of the one being corrected.

Indeed, we may see a logical order here as well: the man of God who brings the Word of God to bear on the congregation will do so in the venue of "sound doctrine" and, as a result, will see that powerful and active Word bringing reproof into the lives of God's people. But it will not stop there: The Word brings correction, restoration, and healing as the Spirit works repentance and a godly commitment to honor Christ. Training in righteousness follows for those who are learning to lay aside the old ways of the flesh and walk in "newness of life" (Romans 6:4). Hence, the entirety of the Christian ministry and life finds its origin, its foundation, its lifeblood, in that which is God-breathed.

These assertions concerning the origin, profitability, and function of the Scriptures, then, provide the basis of the perfection, completion, and equipping of the "man of God" (v. 17). Obviously, the immediate application of Paul's words is to Timothy and his ministry in the church; from Timothy we can extend these truths to all who seek to minister to God's people down through the ages in Christ's church. Note the significant connection between verses 16 and 17: We have seen the high doctrine Paul enunciates about Scripture and its origin, but he also clearly sees this as directly relevant to the work of the ministry. In what sense? "So that the man of God may be *artios*," a Greek term translated as "fully qualified," "proficient," "fully ready," "complete," and "capable." God has given him the tasks of teaching and correcting and training, and if he finds his sufficiency in the God-breathed Scriptures, he will be "fully qualified."

Indeed, Paul adds a second description, "thoroughly equipped."[13] Timothy's competency as the man of God standing upon the Word of God means he will be *completely equipped* for every good work; he will never have to cast about for something to prop him up when he encounters unforeseen circum-

---

[13]From Greek *exartizo*.

stance or difficulty. Each generation of the church has the same promise: When those God calls to serve His people obey Him and rely upon that which He has provided, they will be fully qualified and thoroughly equipped for every good work.[14]

But is there not merit to the objection (raised by many) that if Paul was, in fact, teaching Timothy that the Scriptures are sufficient to equip him for his work in the ministry, that this proves *too* much? In other words, if the Old Testament was "enough," why does he need the New—does this not render the New Testament superfluous? However, such an objection assumes that Paul's intention here is to address the *extent* of Scripture, and there is no evidence that this is the case. Both Paul and Timothy knew they lived in extraordinary times and that the story of Christ was still being recorded under the direction of God for the church's edification.[15] Timothy would not have assumed Paul was even hinting at the issue of the scriptural *canon;* there is no discussion of the canon, the means of recognizing Scripture, or anything of the kind. Paul's meaning is transparent: If it is *theopneustos,* it is Scripture; if it is Scripture, it is profitable. The point is that Scripture's divine origin makes it function as the source for godly ministry and teaching. As the New Testament documents are just as much in the category of *theopneustos* as the Old, Paul's point becomes timeless, relevant for every generation. Surely our discovery of Paul's testimony to the sufficiency of Scripture doesn't prove "too much."

Before moving on to further scriptural testimonies, we should note some of the ramifications of this tremendous passage.[16] If the Scriptures originate in the very breath of Almighty God—that is, if their origin is intimately and essentially *divine*—then their nature cannot be any less than would be commensurate with their source. While *theopneustos* does not speak *first*

---

[14]For a refutation of some leading attempts at undercutting the testimony of this passage, primarily in reference to Roman Catholic apologetics, see King and Webster, *Holy Scripture: The Ground and Pillar of Our Faith,* 1:71–92.

[15]See below, under "Second Peter 1:20–21," for a brief discussion of the evidence that the New Testament writers recognized this work taking place in the lives of others.

[16]2 Timothy 3:16–17.

to nature, it does by logical extension: Since we know that the
Scriptures come from God as from His breath, and that they
are the creation of the Spirit, we are compelled to certain conclusions about their nature.[17] Therefore, when Paul says, "All
Scripture is *theopneustos*" and then goes on to assert Scripture's
ability and capacity to equip the man of God for service in the
church, he is indeed asserting the *sufficiency* of the Scriptures *to
fulfill the purpose God has decreed for them*. And, we have already
seen that if it is a good work in the church, God's people are
"thoroughly equipped" to perform it by referring to the Scriptures. *Almost every sub-Christian and non-Christian theory of ecclesiastical authority, tradition, and extra-biblical "scripture" is refuted by
consideration of Paul's teaching to Timothy in this text.*

Finally, it is profoundly instructive to compare Paul's final
message to Timothy with his words to the Ephesian elders.[18] He
had spent three years with these men, teaching and training
them in the Christian ministry, so a strong parallel exists
between the two situations; in both cases Paul is saying good-
bye to beloved brothers in the service of Christ. Note this
important parallel:

> I know that after my departure savage wolves will come
> in among you, not sparing the flock; and from among your
> own selves men will arise, speaking perverse things, to draw
> away the disciples after them. Therefore be on the alert,
> remembering that night and day for a period of three years
> I did not cease to admonish each one with tears. And now I
> commend you to God and to the word of His grace, which
> is able to build you up and to give you the inheritance
> among all those who are sanctified. (Acts 20:29–32)

Just as Paul warned Timothy of the activities of false teachers, so he sounded the same alarm to the Ephesian elders. In
each scenario one would expect that, upon describing the great
danger and peril facing the infant church, Paul would make
reference to the source, the bulwark, that would protect her
and give these leaders what they needed to press forward and

---

[17]We will expand upon these thoughts throughout this work.
[18]Recorded in Acts 20:17–38.

accomplish the work of ministry. If there *was* to be some external source of authority in the form of the papacy, a group of prophets, new scriptures, or any other extra-scriptural organization or foundation, here is where the apostle would *have* to make mention of it. "Follow Peter's successors in Rome!" "Wait for additional scriptures to be given by God!" "Look to a new generation of prophets God will send!" But Paul says nothing of the sort. Both times, *Paul commits his audience to the Word of God.* Oh, that we would hear and follow today!

SECOND PETER 1:20–21

Just as Paul did not teach Timothy some "new doctrine" when he reminded him of the origin of the Scriptures, so too Peter[19] was simply reflecting the common belief of the apostles when he addressed the same issue in his second epistle. He did so in a similar context, for immediately after addressing the surety of the Scriptures he says, "But false prophets also arose among the people, just as there will also be false teachers among you" (2:1). So once again the question arises in the hearts and minds of God's people: When there are false teachers in the church, how do we distinguish the true from the false? And once again the Bible's answer is not to direct us to some group, or to some extra-biblical body of writings, or to a single charismatic leader. The answer is consistent: God has given us His Word, and that "untaught and unstable" men may distort the Scriptures (3:16) only means there will always be those who *have* been properly taught and instructed and *have* a God-given stability in their handling of the truth who *will* handle the Word aright.

Before Peter begins his lengthy dissertation on the false teachers, he lays the foundation of the divine nature of God's Word:

But know this first of all, that no prophecy of Scripture

---

[19]Many modern commentaries begin with the assumption that, due to its language and content, 2 Peter is not Petrine at all. However, 1 Peter (5:12) specifically mentions an amanuensis (Silvanus), which could explain the rather "classical" flavor of the book's Greek and hence the difference from the style of 2 Peter.

is a matter of one's own interpretation, for no prophecy was
ever made by an act of human will, but men moved by the
Holy Spirit spoke from God. (1:20-21)

Many misread this literal translation as if the focus were on the
individual's interpretation of divine prophecies rather than
upon the origin and nature of the prophecies themselves. Just
before this, Peter speaks of his own experience on the Mount
of Transfiguration, a singular privilege well known by those in
the early church, yet he then says, "We have the prophetic word
made more sure, to which you do well to pay attention as to a
lamp shining in a dark place" (1:19). *He is not talking about how
people interpret the words of prophecy*[20] *but about the certainty of the
Scriptures themselves.* The NIV brings this out with more clarity:

> Above all, you must understand that no prophecy of
> Scripture came about by the prophet's own interpretation.
> For prophecy never had its origin in the will of man, but
> men spoke from God as they were carried along by the Holy
> Spirit.

See as well the rendering of the ESV:

> Knowing this first of all, that no prophecy of Scripture
> comes from someone's own interpretation. For no proph-
> ecy was ever produced by the will of man, but men spoke
> from God as they were carried along by the Holy Spirit.

In both translations the relationship of "interpretation" to
the rest of the verse is more plainly seen. One commentator
has noted regarding the meaning of "interpretation": "releas-
ing, solving, explaining, interpreting. The word almost comes
to mean inspiration. . . . The gen[itive] . . . here indicates
source. Peter is talking about the divine origin of Scripture, not
about its proper interpretation."[21] That this is surely the sense
of the word *interpretation*[22] is seen by its relationship to the

---

[20]"Prophecy" here is used in a much wider sense than a singular prophetic prediction of
   future events; rather, in reference to the Scriptures as a whole.
[21]Cleon Rogers Jr. and Cleon Rogers III, *The New Linguistic and Exegetical Key to the Greek
   New Testament* (Zondervan, 1998), 584.
[22]Greek *epiluseos*.

entire passage. Peter goes on to speak of how the Scriptures came into being, not how they are interpreted, so the meaning of "one's own interpretation" is spelled out in the words that follow: *Scripture is not the opinions of the prophets but the very words of God.* Peter's emphasis is upon denying the human *origin* of the prophetic word, for he goes on to say, "No prophecy was ever made by an act of human will." Men did not wake up one day and decide, "I think I'll write some Scripture." The constantly repeated phrase "The word of the Lord came to me, saying" speaks to this very truth, for in these words the prophet is recognizing that the Lord's words did not come from within but from without. In its prime origination, Scripture is not from the earth but from above.

In contrast to the concept of humanly originated Scripture, Peter asserts that men spoke from God as they were, literally, "carried along" by the Holy Spirit. Does this contradict what was just said? No. Men did speak. Scripture is in human language. It had human authors who were not merely mobile dictation machines. They spoke in their tongue, they spoke from their contexts, they spoke within their cultures, but what they spoke they spoke *from God* and only as they were *carried along* (or *moved*) by the Spirit. Here is the mysterious yet wondrous interface of the human and the divine in Scripture's origination: While men are speaking, they are doing so under the power and direction of the Holy Spirit, so that the result of this divine miracle is, as Paul put it, *God-breathed.* It is not the men themselves who are "inspired" but the Scriptures, the result of this divine initiative in revelation.

Peter roots the certainty of the Word firmly in the sovereign power of God that overrules His creation (cf. Daniel 4:34–35; Psalm 115:3; 135:6). The Spirit carries these men along as He sovereignly chooses, in concert with the divine decree. God determines what He will reveal about Himself, and He gives this revelation in perfection so that these men, despite all their differences and imperfections, give forth only and always what is *from God.* This teaching is perfectly in harmony with what was seen in Paul and is but a reflection of the very views of the Lord

Jesus.[23] Furthermore, do not miss that Peter had already said, "But know this first" (v. 20), literally "knowing this first of all," captured by the NIV's "Above all, you must understand." This is a primary truth, a basic element of sound knowledge of God's work in this world through Christ. If you do not first recognize the divine nature of Scripture, you will easily fall prey to the false teachers Peter is about to excoriate. Those who lightly dismiss inspiration and inerrancy do so directly in opposition to apostolic wisdom and apostolic command.

One last comment on Peter's view of Scripture: Given the tremendously high view he teaches, it is all the more amazing that later in this epistle he makes reference to some of the letters of his fellow apostle and includes them as "Scripture"!

> Regard the patience of our Lord to be salvation; just as also our beloved brother Paul, according to the wisdom given him, wrote to you, as also in all his letters, speaking in them of these things, in which are some things hard to understand, which the untaught and unstable distort, as they do also the rest of the Scriptures, to their own destruction. (3:15–16)

In speaking of the "rest of the Scriptures," Peter is pointedly acknowledging that the Spirit is once again bringing Scripture into existence. Paul likewise references the words of Luke's gospel as Scripture in 1 Timothy 5:18, so it follows that the apostles knew God was at work in providing the church with the new covenant Scriptures; surely the Scriptures presenting the fulfillment of God's work in Christ would share the high divine nature inherent within those of the old covenant.

MATTHEW 22:29–32

Thus far we have seen two apostles teaching the same truth concerning the divine origin and nature of the Word. What can explain the harmony of their teachings? The Holy Spirit speaks harmoniously, and hence we can expect such consistency, which it seems is likewise found in that both men are reflecting

---

[23]See below, under "Matthew 22:29–32."

the views of the Lord Jesus Himself. Though a full accounting of the tremendously high view of Scripture found throughout Jesus' teachings is beyond our scope, one particular passage stands out not only for its forcefulness but also because it is often missed in our reading of the gospel narratives.

I refer to His response to the question asked by the Sadducees in Matthew 22. Here we find the Sadducees (who did *not* believe in the resurrection) attempting to confound Him with a story that had obviously served them well in various street-corner debates they'd undertaken against the Pharisees (who *did* believe in the resurrection). They speak of a woman who successively married seven brothers; after they all died, she too died—to whom would she be married in heaven? The scenario was meant to put the defender of the resurrection in the impossible position of explaining postmortem marriage practices without any divine revelation touching upon the subject. Jesus' response was both compelling and "politically incorrect."

> "You are mistaken, not understanding the Scriptures nor the power of God. For in the resurrection they neither marry nor are given in marriage, but are like angels in heaven.
> But regarding the resurrection of the dead, have you not read what was spoken to you by God: 'I AM THE GOD OF ABRAHAM, AND THE GOD OF ISAAC, AND THE GOD OF JACOB'? He is not the God of the dead but of the living" (vv. 29–32).

The Lord's reply is quick and crushing. "You are mistaken" signals that He has no intention of playing their semantic games. He informs them that they understand neither the Scriptures nor the power of God; obviously, this means that if they did understand these things, they could arrive at a true knowledge. Nevertheless, despite their extensive learning, they are in error. They do not realize that the resurrection marks a major transition, and that their insistence upon knowing about subsequent marital arrangements has led them astray. The Scriptures had already revealed to them that God is the God of the *living;* Abraham, Isaac, and Jacob were all in the presence of God, alive. That the people are astonished at His response indicates that the Pharisees had never come up with this response to the Sadducees' trap.

However, even in summarizing the text we skipped over one of the strongest affirmations of Scripture's divine nature without even noting it. The words do not scream out for attention, and since they are said in passing, we tend to miss them. Listen again to what the Lord said to the Sadducees: "Have you not read what was spoken to you by God?" Consider the oddity of this phrase: Generally, after "have you not read," we would expect the next phrase to be "what was *written* to you?" When we see "what was spoken to you," we expect to have heard it in the context of "Did you not *hear*?" But Jesus mixes these terms: "Have you not *read* what was *spoken* to you by God?"

Why does He do this? The answer is not difficult to find. When the Lord asked His opponents if they had *read* what God said to them, He was making reference to the reading of the Scriptures; He went on to cite from Exodus 3:6. His words "what was spoken to you by God" enunciate the same truth we saw in Paul: *Scripture is God speaking.* Though the words they'd read had been penned more than a thousand years earlier, still God *spoke* in the reading of those words. Jesus held them accountable for the words of Scripture as if God Himself had spoken those words directly to them! Such an attitude on the Lord's part would be unthinkable *unless* the Scriptures are in fact the very embodiment of the eternal God speaking to us across the vistas of time.

Only the very highest view of Scripture could possibly stand behind these words, which is exactly what we find when we consider His reverence for and use of Scripture. When facing Jews who wished to stone Him for blasphemy, and quoting from the Old Testament in such a fashion as to identify His accusers as false, unrighteous judges, Jesus repeated the profession of all of God's people: "The Scripture cannot be broken" (John 10:35). The fulfillment of prophecy is a given in the Gospels, and the mere citation of "Thus saith the Lord" is enough to establish any point in the Lord's ministry.

THE HUMAN EQUATION: LUKE 1:3–4

It is extremely popular in modern theology to emphasize the human nature of Scripture. Unfortunately, this is often at the expense of its divine nature, resulting in the diminishment of the Bible's own teaching about itself. In a very large portion of "Christendom" today, the Bible is an important, quasi-authoritative collection of thoughts about God that, while once thought to be inspired and inerrant, has been "discovered" to be "far more human" than previously perceived. While we reject the unbelieving skepticism of postmodernism that rules and reigns in so many quarters, we surely cannot go to the *other* extreme and make the Scriptures "docetic" by denying their human element. Our insistence is that the human element does not introduce into the nature of Scripture what liberal theologians demand: the existence of error. God's work of inspiration is not limited by every author He used being sinful, imperfect, and ignorant of many things. This is why we must note again that *Scripture* is "inspired" ("God-breathed"), *not those whom God used to write it.* Their humanity is not the foundation of the Word; it is a tool God used that did not in any way limit the perfection of the masterpiece that came from His hand.

An illustration of the human element that points to Scripture's accuracy and reliability is provided by the pen of Luke, who introduces his gospel to Theophilus by stating,

> It seemed fitting for me as well, having investigated everything carefully from the beginning, to write it out for you in consecutive order, most excellent Theophilus; so that you may know the exact truth about the things you have been taught. (1:3–4)

These words do not mesh well with a postmodern perspective on religion; they sound far more like a scientist speaking about the results of his studies. Postmodernism accepts assured results regarding physics or medicine (for example) but denies the same kind of certainty regarding the spiritual realm (due to the assumption that, unlike the clarity that comes from naturalistic experimentation and study, there is no corresponding divine revelation that can give us a knowledge of the truth). But Luke was not a postmodernist, and he claims that what he is writing is not only the result of careful investigation but that the result is also something that will allow Theophilus "to know the exact truth about the things you have been taught." Exact truth, not a facsimile thereof; not a close approximation, not a good guess, but *the exact truth.* The ESV renders it "that you may have certainty," and this is the problem for many of today's interpreters: Certainty in religious matters is assumed to be an impossible goal, so even the explicit claims of the biblical writers have to be questioned and then rejected.

These words from Luke speak to the human element in Scripture. The stories he relates, the events he records, he investigated, researched, and then wrote. He exercised his mind and engaged in careful study; he did not just sit down one day and begin to write. Now, obviously, there are sections of Scripture that were written in a different fashion, prophecies recorded that came suddenly to the writers. Elsewhere the biblical writer will speak of his personal experiences, his desires, his feelings of abandonment, or his need to have his brothers and sisters pray for him. Scripture records a wide range of human emotion, but there is no contradiction between the activity of the human writers in researching, seeking prayer, or even crying out in despair, joy, or anger, and the work of the Spirit in molding these human experiences (which are, after all, under the sovereign decree of God) into the very revelation He intended His church to possess and obey. The God who spoke and created all things can surely bring His Word into existence in the fashion He chooses without introducing into it error and blemish.

CHAPTER 4

Inerrancy and Exegesis: Believing and Honoring God's Word

At first glance, this portion of this book may seem to be "skippable." If you already believe in inerrancy, you might regard discussion of it as extraneous; interesting, but not really necessary. Furthermore, "exegesis" is hardly a term that causes heart-pounding excitement in the pews of most modern churches. Even so, this chapter contains some of the most important truths about the means by which we know God's truth and can have faith in His revelation.

A word of warning right up front: While what is said here may sound standard to many readers, the foundations upon which my position stands are no longer accepted in a large portion of what is called "Christian academia." For many, the so-called battle for inerrancy was fought and won at the end of the twentieth century, but in my experience this is wishful thinking. While many today might *say* they believe in inerrancy, the fact is that few truly embrace it as central and definitional. Inerrancy has been so redefined that its real meaning has been lost, which can be seen in that many theologians who sign statements or membership pledges that include "inerrancy" will also espouse theologies that clearly propound "tension in the text" (a quaint buzz-phrase that means "contradiction") and that make no sense outside of a rejection of inerrancy's historical definition.

Many scholars do not find inerrancy a sufficiently important reason to avoid the newest trends in theology and step outside the accepted bounds of "the academy." Let's face it: Maintaining inerrancy in European theological circles is as popular as espousing belief in a flat earth; the situation is only slightly better in America. Theology here is following society's path, being far more influenced by the culture than by the abiding and unchanging Word. The perceived cutting edge of theology abandoned belief in inerrancy a long time ago.

But I truly do not have great sadness at waving "so long" to the academy on this issue. Church history has repeatedly and clearly proven one thing: Once the highest view of Scripture is abandoned by any theologian, group, denomination, or church, the downhill slide in both its theology and practice is inevitable. I firmly believe Christian truth requires a solid foundation in the beliefs that (1) God made us, and (2) God has communicated to us with clarity. Without this basis, attempts to establish Christian theology are untenable.

No wonder, then, that confusion reigns supreme in many quarters today. The wide-ranging beliefs in so many churches and denominations are not due to any fault in the Scriptures but rather to people rejecting the ultimate authority of God's Word, either by denying its accuracy (and hence its teachings) or by subjecting it to a higher functional authority (such as the tradition of an "infallible" group or person).

HOW DID WE GET WHERE WE ARE?

This point was glowingly illustrated a number of years ago as I stood passing out tracts on the sidewalk outside the Easter pageant of the LDS Church in Mesa, Arizona. A young man who walked by and took a tract immediately looked at it as he was moving away, then stopped. I could sense the struggle in his body language: "Do I go back and talk to these folks, or just keep going?" The enticement got the better of him, and his first question was most interesting: "Why are there so many Christian churches today?"

I explained that there are two main reasons, one legitimate and one not. The *legitimate* reason is that God does not make us in a cookie-cutter fashion; therefore, each fellowship has its own character, and there are elements of worship and practice wherein godly people can differ. However, the *illegitimate* reason is this: People pick and choose which portions of the Bible they will believe and which they will not.

He didn't seem impressed with my response, but we progressed to other issues. Quickly the topic of salvation came up, and given that he was very sharp, he saw that the message of free grace I was proclaiming undercut his own ideas of the necessity of works. He asked if I was saying we are saved by grace alone without works, and, if so, doesn't it mean that God is the one choosing who will be saved? I opened my Bible to Ephesians 1:11 and read the following:

> In whom also we have obtained an inheritance, being predestinated according to the purpose of him who worketh all things after the counsel of his own will. (KJV)

He listened and then began, "So you believe—"
I stopped him mid-sentence and reread the text.
"So you are saying—"
Again I stopped him and reread the text.
At this point he looked over the top of my Bible, found the text, tapped it with his index finger, and said, "That is wrong, and I feel good saying that."

I closed my Bible, buttoned the flap, looked at him, and replied, "When you first walked up to me, you asked why there are so many Christian churches. I told you then that the main reason is people picking and choosing which parts of the Bible they will believe and which they will not. No one, sir, has given me a better example of that than you just did."

Without a firm foundation, a discernable standard, an unchanging and unchangeable rule, we are left to construct a theology that can ascend no higher than majority opinion, that cannot claim divine authority (though this may not keep such a system from claiming such), and that can only replace the divine consistency of Scripture with its own supposed inherent authority. Men's traditions, even if called "the Word of God," are insufficient to replace the consistent testimony of the divinely inspired, harmonious, inerrant Scriptures. In other words, without the highest view of Scripture, we can never claim to have heard from God with certainty, and hence we cannot teach and preach with any more authority than that which we can create for ourselves.

INERRANCY DEFINED:
THE CHICAGO STATEMENT ON INERRANCY

In 1978 a group of widely recognized evangelical scholars and writers met in Chicago and produced a clear, concise statement on the meaning and importance of inerrancy with reference to biblical authority. As we touch on many of these issues elsewhere, we will not reproduce the entire statement but will focus upon those passages that help in defining inerrancy's key elements.

ARTICLE II

We affirm that the Scriptures are the supreme written norm by which God binds the conscience, and that the authority of the Church is subordinate to that of Scripture.

We deny that church creeds, councils, or declarations have authority greater than or equal to the authority of the Bible.

The statement begins with an affirmation of Scripture's supreme authority, derived from its inspired nature. Since Scripture is God-breathed, it cannot admit to equal authorities not breathed out by God. Thus the negative statement is actually a denial that churches, creeds, councils, etc., are themselves God-breathed and that they must have, at best, a derivative nature.

ARTICLE III

> We affirm that the written Word in its entirety is revelation given by God.
> We deny that the Bible is merely a witness to revelation, or only becomes revelation in encounter, or depends on the responses of men for its validity.

This article speaks to the widely held idea that the Bible is not, in its very nature, revelation from God, but is something less. Some view it merely as a *witness to revelation* that transcends written words. It is also common to believe that the Bible *becomes* the Word of God when we *encounter* it in our own lives, as if its nature is dependent upon the experiences of its readers! The problem is that those who propound such views will nevertheless use the same terminology as past generations, referring to the Bible as "God's Word" and affirming its "authority." As a result, *God's people are often confused by teachers who say they believe the Bible is God's Word but then deny this through holding to theologies inconsistent with such a confession.* "How can he believe that?" is the question I hear all the time, and in the majority of instances the reason for odd, unbiblical teachings flows directly from holding errant views of scriptural authority.

ARTICLE IV

> We affirm that God who made mankind in His image has used language as a means of revelation.
> We deny that human language is so limited by our creatureliness that it is rendered inadequate as a vehicle for divine revelation. We further deny that the corruption of human culture and language through sin has thwarted God's work of inspiration.

This article responds to those who propound a diminishment in biblical authority based upon the alleged inability of language to convey truth effectively. God created man in His image and gave to man the capacity to communicate. Speech is truly a gift from God, and though man's fall into sin *impacts* his ability to communicate and understand, it does not *destroy* that ability. God considers speech a sufficient basis for communication, so we should as well.

ARTICLE V

> We affirm that God's revelation in the Holy Scriptures
> was progressive.
> We deny that later revelation, which may fulfill earlier
> revelation, ever corrects or contradicts it. We further deny
> that any normative revelation has been given since the com-
> pletion of the New Testament writings.

"Progressive revelation" simply means that God did not drop a completed, finished revelation from heaven in a single gold-covered package. Primary and basic truths (such as monotheism, the belief in one God) were revealed first, with further truths uncovered for us at later points. Asserting that God has indeed revealed things over time does not necessitate that the later revelations correct, abrogate, or contradict the earlier ones. (This is important in dealing with objections to the New Testament in light of traditional Jewish beliefs regarding the content and meaning of the Old Testament.) The article's final denial likewise separates the biblical authors from all modern groups (such as the Church of Jesus Christ of Latter-day Saints) that purport to possess "new revelations" comprising an expanded canon.

ARTICLE VI

> We affirm that the whole of Scripture and all its parts,
> down to the very words of the original, were given by divine
> inspiration.
> We deny that the inspiration of Scripture can rightly be
> affirmed of the whole without the parts, or of some parts
> but not the whole.

Here we begin to encounter the doctrine of inerrancy at its very base. Many wish to limit "inspiration" to the whole of Scripture without affirming it of the individual parts. That is, one can say "John's gospel is inspired" without also saying that, say, John 10 and its teaching about Christ's sheep is itself inspired and inerrant. Accordingly, one is always left wondering which parts are inspired and which are not . . . so some external authority must come in to make heads or tails of the Bible. That authority can be tradition or, in the more liberal denominations, personal experience and encounter with the Word. "I *feel* that this part is really inspired" is obviously a problematic basis for Christian theology.

ARTICLE VII

We affirm that inspiration was the work in which God by His Spirit, through human writers, gave us His Word. The origin of Scripture is divine. The mode of divine inspiration remains largely a mystery to us.

We deny that inspiration can be reduced to human insight, or to heightened states of consciousness of any kind.

This article takes us back to Paul and Warfield and *theopneustos* and Peter and holy men speaking from God. It is meant to affirm Scripture's divine nature while denying that inspiration is merely a heightened level of understanding or a deeper spiritual sense of God's presence in the writing of these books (commonly held views).

ARTICLE VIII

We affirm that God in His work of inspiration utilized the distinctive personalities and literary styles of the writers whom He had chosen and prepared.

We deny that God, in causing these writers to use the very words that He chose, overrode their personalities.

This is a vital affirmation and denial. Some people confuse the confession of *plenary, verbal* inspiration with the *verbal dictation theory* of inspiration. When we confess that the Bible is inspired and inerrant in its entirety and to the level of the words used in the text, we do not have to embrace the idea that the writers were merely human dictation machines, engaging in some sort of "automatic writing" while entranced. It is clear that they were fully engaged in their task, expressing their own feelings in their own words, their own tongues, their own dialects; Paul's grammar, style, and choice of words are quite different than that of Luke or of John. The various writers of the Psalms likewise show variance of style. The dictation theory, which holds that the authors' wills were overridden to the point of there being no human component in the writing of the Scriptures, cannot account for the very *human* outcry of Paul, "Brethren, pray for us!" (1 Thessalonians 5:25), or for the wretched, soul-wracked despair of the psalmist in Psalm 88.

At the same time, though, we need not abandon our belief in the inspiration of the very *words* of Scripture. The same God who created all things, who upholds all things by the word of His power, who made the mind and tongue of man, and who works all things after the counsel of His will, is able to decree both the ends (the final form of Scripture, to its very text) and the means (the experiences and contexts and languages of the men He used). Can *we* record this divine process on film, chart it, demonstrate it through some kind of electronic instrument? Surely not, but a God who by speaking can create light itself is not beyond using His creation in such a fashion.

ARTICLE IX

We affirm that inspiration, though not conferring omniscience, guaranteed true and trustworthy utterance on all matters of which the Biblical authors were moved to speak and write.

We deny that the finitude or falseness of these writers, by necessity or otherwise, introduced distortion or falsehood into God's Word.

It is commonly argued that the Scriptures cannot be inerrant because the instruments used to record them (sinful men lacking omniscience) would by necessity twist and distort the message. But this is little more than a claim that the omniscient and omnipotent God is incapable of using even the fallen creation to accomplish the ends of His divine decree. Was God truly dependent upon the omniscience of the authors in giving His Word? Remember: Men spoke *from* God as they were *carried along* by the Holy Spirit (2 Peter 1:20–21). Does it not follow that the Spirit would never carry these men into error? Would not the need for omniscience be only on the part of the Spirit? The belief that imperfect humans necessarily preclude an inerrant revelation is based primarily upon a rejection of God's sovereignty in human affairs. The God who knows every word we speak before we speak it (Psalm 139:4) is capable of superintending a divine process so that what is spoken is done willingly on the part of the speaker and yet the result is exactly as God decreed it.

ARTICLE XI

We affirm that Scripture, having been given by divine inspiration, is infallible, so that, far from misleading us, it is true and reliable in all the matters it addresses.

We deny that it is possible for the Bible to be at the same time infallible and errant in its assertions. Infallibility and inerrancy may be distinguished but not separated.

Some make a great show of saying the Scriptures are infallible while questioning whether they are inerrant (or whether we can know they are inerrant). That is, they say that while what the Scriptures *lead us to believe* is infallibly true, *the means by which this takes place* (especially in regard to the actual text of Scripture) can be errant. Hence the article's words: "We deny that it is possible for the Bible to be at the same time infallible and errant in its assertions." For a reason that honestly escapes me, some evangelicals like to embrace "tension" so as to hold internally incoherent views, as if this alleged mystery is a good and godly thing that allows them to avoid being "too dogmatic" about things. They find it attractive to be able to say the Bible is infallible in its teaching (and limiting the realm of that teaching to the "spiritual") while not having to be labeled an ignorant fundamentalist for believing it to be inerrant. The problem, of course, is that this makes no sense. *Infallible teaching is not derived from errant foundations.*

ARTICLE XII

We affirm that Scripture in its entirety is inerrant, being free from all falsehood, fraud, or deceit.

We deny that Biblical infallibility and inerrancy are limited to spiritual, religious, or redemptive themes, exclusive of assertions in the fields of history and science. We further deny that scientific hypotheses about earth history may properly be used to overturn the teaching of Scripture on creation and the flood.

Here the framers of the statement touch upon the rub of inerrancy: for many, the doctrine "simply cannot survive in a scientific age." That is, they see it as a dinosaur from the past, a belief that could have held plausibility for those who did not understand the ramifications of technological and scientific advancement (macroevolution, modern cosmologies, etc.) but that must be abandoned to remain "rational" in today's context. For many this is an overwhelming argument that leads them to hold on to a form of scriptural authority that is limited to the "spiritual realm." Supposedly, the Bible may be wrong about miracles or cosmology or creation, but it can safely be trusted in "spiritual matters." Of course, this results in a complete disassociation of the "spiritual" from "everything else," leaving these teachings hanging in midair with no foundation but feelings.

There is no question that Christians have sometimes extended the biblical text far beyond its scope in order to promote any number of sometimes fantastic theories and beliefs (regarding cosmology, for example), but such is hardly relevant to the actual validity of the biblical text. *The misuse of an inerrant source does not render it errant.* Many enemies of the faith have concluded that since unfounded ideas that once claimed biblical support have been refuted, the Bible itself has been refuted. The framers here refute this assumption.

ARTICLE XIII

We affirm the propriety of using inerrancy as a theological term with reference to the complete truthfulness of Scripture.

We deny that it is proper to evaluate Scripture according to standards of truth and error that are alien to its usage or purpose. We further deny that inerrancy is negated by Biblical phenomena such as a lack of modern technical precision, irregularities of grammar or spelling, observational descriptions of nature, the reporting of falsehoods, the use of hyperbole and round numbers, the topical arrangement of metrical, variant selections of material in parallel accounts, or the use of free citations.

How do the denials of this article fit with its affirmation? In essence, many will not hold to inerrancy *because* at some level they are convinced that the Bible contains errors in the categories presented in the article's denial section. As we will note repeatedly when we later speak to the issue of alleged contradictions,[1] the testing of Scripture's claims on the basis of a foreign standard, context, or worldview usually lies behind allegations of error. So the positive affirmation is that we can indeed use the term *inerrancy,* for when we recognize all the errors men promulgate through their errant analysis of Scripture, based upon false standards, we find no reason *not* to maintain inerrancy.

Each of the categories (listed in the article's denial section) is indeed important: It is obviously insignificant to say, "Well, you don't get the exact definition of pi [3.141592654= ...] when you look at 1 Kings 7:23 and see that the round object there is ten cubits across and thirty around." Yet it is this kind of insistence upon modern scientific precision that is demanded by many who deny inerrancy. Further, questions such as whether a writer used what we would consider correct grammar or spelling or whether one should say "the sun rose" frequently appear in literature critical of inerrancy. All of these concepts will be treated in our defense of inerrancy later in this work.[2]

ARTICLE XIV

We affirm the unity and internal consistency of Scripture.

We deny that alleged errors and discrepancies that have

---

[1]See chapter 8.
[2]See chapters 7 and 8.

not yet been resolved violate the truth claims of the Bible.

How can one seriously believe in inerrancy if there are *errors and discrepancies that have not yet been resolved?* Because of the nature of the text we are examining. There have been many past instances where people thought for certain they had convicted God's Word of error *based upon the current state of knowledge in their day,* only to be proven wrong in succeeding generations. Growth in knowledge of the historical context, cultures, events, and languages brought vindication of the text. Was the text wrong when believers lacked the background information by which to fully clarify a text? Not at all—the error lay in the ignorance of the critic. Hence, if the document's track record is such that it has repeatedly vindicated itself, when alleged errors or discrepancies stem from a lack of background information upon which to fully contextualize the situation, we are perfectly justified in saying that our ignorance does not deny the inerrancy of the text.

ARTICLE XV

We affirm that the doctrine of inerrancy is grounded in the teaching of the Bible about inspiration.

We deny that Jesus' teaching about Scripture may be dismissed by appeals to accommodation or to any natural limitation of His humanity.

One of the most truly amazing results of humanist and postmodernist encroachment into the realm of Christian theology and ministry is the specter of a Christian minister or teacher who stands before God's people and while confessing (in the words of the ancient creeds) belief in the deity and resurrection of Christ teaches and preaches a view of the Scriptures utterly contrary to that found throughout the length and breadth of the teaching ministry of Jesus Himself. What an absurdity to say you trust Christ to raise you from the dead but do not trust His own view of the Scriptures. And yet in many a seminary today men stand before their classes and dismiss Jesus' tremendously high doctrine of Scripture by saying that His view was merely an "accommodation" to the simplistic worldview of His listeners, or that possibly He really believed these things but this was part of the "self-emptying" involved in the Incarnation so that His knowledge was not up to speed. Why anyone would wish to entrust their eternity to someone unfamiliar with the real nature of God's Word, I cannot begin to imagine.

Then again, without a reliable, inspired record of what Christ did, and the reasons for His sacrifice, who can truly know what it means to believe the gospel anyway? The certainty of the revelation is *foundational* to the proclamation of the gospel. Without inspiration and inerrancy, the gospel of power becomes a suggestion of weakness.

ARTICLE XVI

> We affirm that the doctrine of inerrancy has been integral to the Church's faith throughout its history.
>
> We deny that inerrancy is a doctrine invented by scholastic Protestantism, or is a reactionary position postulated in response to negative higher criticism.

History can be a great guide or a great deceiver, depending on how careful we are in its use. Each generation has its own set of concerns, battles, and disputes. We often mistreat those who came before by trying to force their words to address our questions. The fact that the Scriptures have been believed to be the very speaking of God, without error, without falsehood, by Christians down through the centuries seems difficult to deny. But since that was the case, addressing particular objections to inerrancy that flow from contemporary philosophy or science would not have been a part of the church's experience in preceding centuries. Hence, we should not be surprised if the writings of those generations do not clearly address some of the subjects *we* would like to see addressed. This does not make inerrancy a merely modern belief any more than not seeing discussions of genetic engineering in the third century means early Christians were accepting of it; it had no place in their experience.

ARTICLE XVII

We affirm that the Holy Spirit bears witness to the Scriptures, assuring believers of the truthfulness of God's written Word.

We deny that this witness of the Holy Spirit operates in isolation from or against Scripture.

Some find *sola scriptura* to be stifling to the Spirit, as if having a firm, unchanging, clear, understandable revelation from God means the Spirit is now irrelevant. The Word can be as plain as day, but without the Spirit's work in the heart to bring about obedience, there will be no faith, no repentance, no understanding. "The Word and the Spirit" is a phrase found throughout Christian history in the writings of those who understood the vital union of the Holy Spirit and the Word He birthed into existence. Nevertheless, the order must be kept straight: It is not my Spirit-borne feelings that *make* the Scriptures true; they are what they are *in and of themselves*. They were true before I was born; they will be true long after I am gone. My obedient understanding of them, my faith in them, my trust in their message, requires a work of their Author, the Spirit, and that mainly because of a deficiency that exists in me: my sin, my ignorance. I am dependent upon the Spirit for the positive affirmation that exists in my heart regarding the teaching and message of Scripture.

At the same time, the denial element of this article is vitally important as well. If the Spirit does not act in concert with the Word, how can He be called the Spirit of truth?[3] Many today do not believe it is God's purpose for the Spirit to work in concert with the Word, instead insisting that the Spirit can work separately from the Word in giving separate revelatory knowledge. Since this is a common belief, we will address it in a later dialogue.[4]

ARTICLE XVIII

We affirm that the text of Scripture is to be interpreted by grammatico-historical exegesis, taking account of its lit-

---

[3] Cf. John 14:17.
[4] See chapter 10.

erary forms and devices, and that Scripture is to interpret Scripture.

We deny the legitimacy of any treatment of the text or quest for sources lying behind it that leads to relativizing, dehistoricizing, or discounting its teaching, or rejecting its claims of authorship.

This article touches upon a central aspect of what I have come to believe is elementary to all sound theology and proclamation: Inerrancy is the foundation of sound exegesis; exegesis is the means by which we honor God in His Word. Deny inerrancy, and the authority of the Word disintegrates. Deny the ability of exegesis to sufficiently communicate the original meaning and intention of the authors, and again, the authority of the Word disintegrates as external sources must be brought in to "clarify" the truth. This is taking place all around us, even in denominations and groups that were once focused upon the meat of the gospel, in the forefront of the battle, but are now off on some tangent, sidetracked from the main and plain things. Entire denominations have been laid waste by embracing some quest for an extra-biblical view of Christ and the gospel events. The popularity of liberal theories resulting in the "demythologizing" of the gospels (specifically) and the Scriptures (generally) has lead to complete confusion and uncertainty regarding the Christian faith and the gospel message.

ARTICLE XIX

We affirm that a confession of the full authority, infallibility and inerrancy of Scripture is vital to a sound understanding of the whole of the Christian faith. We further affirm that such confession should lead to increasing conformity to the image of Christ.

We deny that such confession is necessary for salvation. However, we further deny that inerrancy can be rejected without grave consequences, both to the individual and to the Church.

This article provides a fitting conclusion to our review of the statement and of inerrancy's definition. As the denial states, *inerrancy is not part of the gospel message.* That is, there are believers who, due to their tradition, the influence of someone important in their lives, or any other reason(s), muddle along believing the Bible to be untrustworthy in some aspect or another. And yet they know and love Christ, trusting Him solely for their salvation.

On the other hand, sound Christian theology suffers a slow and horrible death in those churches and denominations where the theories of men take precedence over the authority of Scripture. When inerrancy is denied (openly or functionally), the foundation of theology is removed, and nothing people have found can replace it. It may take time, but *the denigration of Christian truth that flows from the abandonment of the highest views of Scripture is simply inevitable.* It cannot be avoided.

EXEGESIS: LETTING GOD SPEAK

In vitally important ways it is a science, requiring of its regular and careful practitioner painstaking attention to detail and the utilization of the tools of his trade. In other ways it is an art, something at which one becomes ever more skilled with practice and the passage of time. In other aspects it is an act of worship, requiring spiritual preparation and a willing heart marked by obedience. For some it is a nuisance, something only "elitists" do to prove their theologies. And then there are those who find it nothing more than a chore, something to be done because it needs to be done, though it fires no passions and doesn't engage the heart or mind.

I am referring to *exegesis,* the process of seeking to understand the written text of Scripture in its own context. Believing, committed exegesis is a rare skill these days, for it requires the highest view of Scripture coupled with a deep and abiding desire to obey the Word in all of its aspects. While a person may possess the technical skills (knowledge of the ancient languages, ability to follow grammar, and so on) to exegete, *believing exegesis* of God's Word goes beyond this level to that of the heart. A believing exegete is not content with successfully working through all the issues that can surround a difficult text;

instead, he wishes to come to a sound conclusion *for a purpose,* ultimately, for the glory of the God he believes revealed the text and for his own growth in the grace and knowledge of the Lord Jesus Christ.

Exegesis can be defined with reference to its opposite: *eisegesis.* To exegete a passage is to *lead the native meaning out from the words;* to eisegete a passage is to *insert a foreign meaning into the words.* You are exegeting a passage when you are allowing it to say *what its original author intended;* you are eisegeting a passage when you are forcing the author to say *what you want the author to say.* True exegesis shows respect for the text and, by extension, for its author; eisegesis, even when based upon ignorance, shows disrespect for the text and its author.

Exegesis involves work. There are rules that govern the process, most of which we know by instinct and some of which we must learn. Most of us know that when we read someone else's writings, we should exercise *some* effort to determine what *they* were trying to say. When our parents told us, "Clean your room," we knew it would not have gotten us very far to say, "Yeah, but I thought you meant 'clean your room next year.'" That would have involved gross eisegesis, inserting a concept that was not only absent from the original *command* but was obviously contradicted by the *context* as well. Children don't need graduate study in exegesis to know when they are avoiding the plain meaning of something.

Every day we practice exegesis, for when we read or listen to anything, we have to apply a set of rules so as to interpret what has been said or written. How often do we have to complain, "But you took that out of context!" when someone misrepresents or misunderstands our intentions? How often is something we wrote in an e-mail or a letter misconstrued by someone who *wanted* to think we were saying something else? In these cases we are talking about merely human writing or merely human communication.

So what is involved in doing sound exegesis? Entire works exist on the subject, from varied perspectives; many are excellent resources, some are not.[5] One must look carefully to the viewpoints of the author(s) regarding scriptural inspiration and inerrancy. Even some that do not hold the highest views can provide useful information in other areas; discernment is the key. Here we'll go through a brief synopsis before getting to the real issue regarding exegesis and biblical sufficiency.

THE RULES OF EXEGESIS

Fundamentally, the rules of exegesis exist to protect the text; that is, if we want to know what the text meant originally, we must protect it from misinterpretation in the form of eisegesis. We need to follow these rules so that we do not read into the text anachronistic meanings unreflective of the author's meaning. In the study of Scripture, the overall field we are touching upon here is called *hermeneutics*.

The vast majority of these rules relates to one thing: Written documents communicate through *context*. While individual words carry meaning, that meaning is often narrowed and focused through the use of context. Nearly every aspect of serious exegesis is related to the proper handling of context, and nearly every example of erroneous interpretation involves a violation of the context of the original document. As we now look at some of the major issues in exegesis, note how every one of them involves context.

Author

Who is the author? What do we know about him? Can we identify his origins, his background? What can we learn about the elements that influenced him? Obviously, the more someone knows about you as a person, the better they can evaluate your writing. A close friend can decipher even the most quickly jotted note, while someone lacking personal knowledge of you may be utterly incapable of knowing what you meant. Hence, the more we know about the author and his lineage, culture, language, and worldview, the better we can handle his words in the way they were intended. Obviously we know *some* of the biblical authors, but other entire works are anonymous. When we

---

[5]A tremendously useful bibliography on this issue can be found in Grant Osborne's *The Hermeneutical Spiral* (InterVarsity Press, 1991), 436–80.

do not know an author, we may be able at least to identify the time range in which he wrote and the social milieu that provides the background.

Audience

To whom was the author writing? Is there a specific audience (such as when Paul wrote to the church at Corinth or to Timothy), or is the work more general in scope (such as 1 Chronicles or the Psalms)? Was there a specific historical set of circumstances that prompted the writing? How does the audience's cultural context influence the writing? Does the writer make reference to commonly held beliefs or experiences that we might not immediately understand? *Many* questions can be asked of the relationship between author and audience that impact how we comprehend particular textual elements; ignoring these elements and transporting the biblical author and audience into a modern context is one of the most common errors leading to eisegetical misinterpretation. Assuming the ancient writer would "think like me" on this or that issue is one of the main reasons modern preaching so often turns ancient writers into postmodern Americans rather than allowing them to speak within their intended context.

Historical Setting

What was going on in the world in which the author and his audience lived? What about the government at the time? Would these facts be relevant to comments made in the text? For example, how often is the political situation in Israel or Judah relevant to the meaning of the Old Testament prophets? How often does Rome loom large over the Gospels or the Pauline epistles?

Issues of background and setting are often lumped together under certain German terms that serve little use other than to make it seem like you need to attend seminary to understand these issues. *Sitz im Leben* (i.e., the locale of interpretation, the place and context in which the document would be read and initially interpreted) and *Weltanshauung* (worldview), for instance, pepper scholarly documents primarily because they give the appearance of scholarship. The serious student of

Scripture can fully appreciate the need to consider the factors that go into determining the specific textual background, regardless of whether or not he's learned theological German and can translate such phrases.

Lexicography

Lexicography refers to the study of the meaning of words. Here, considering the exact form of the text, we pass from background issues to those where the battle is often fought with greatest ferocity. Remarkable strides have been taken in this field during recent centuries, and the Bible student today has greater access to fine lexical sources than any preceding generation. We choose the words we do for a particular purpose, and we must always ask, "Why did the author utilize this particular term? What did it mean to him? Why not use a synonym? Is this particular usage truly significant?" The study of lexical semantics has opened up broad vistas for carefully representing the intention of the original text regarding word choice.

Grammar

Grammar is often where the reader's eyes become glassy, for many will confess that the term raises all sorts of unpleasant memories from their educational past. However, the words used by the writer are the vehicles of meaning, and by selecting their forms and arrangements he intends to communicate in a *particular* fashion. Any claimed interpretation of the text that does not even bother dealing with the actual *form* of the text, down to whether the writer uses a verb in one tense, or a noun in another case, is not really an interpretation at all. We choose our words so as to communicate our meaning, even if we cannot specifically label the grammatical forms we are using. This is a foundational part of the process.

Consider the grammar of Isaiah 9:6 and the description of the coming Messiah as "Mighty God." Look at the importance of the use of the term *Deity* in Colossians 2:9, or the contrast of verbal forms that carries so much weight in the prologue of John. Consider almost any relevant biblical text: Somewhere along the line, its grammar will take center stage in providing the key element of properly understanding its meaning.

Textual Issues

This refers to the fact that both Testaments contain textual variations due to scribal errors, and at times these can impact the possible range of meanings to be assigned to the passage. Ignore this element of the study and you'll encounter the problem many preachers face today: preaching on a passage only to discover that half their audience, due to the use of a different translation, doesn't even have in their Bibles the key phrase upon which the minister is focused! This frequent occurrence is both distracting and disturbing to the listeners.

Syntax

Syntax refers to the relationship the words of the text have to each other, taking into consideration their grammatical forms. This is the next step up from consideration of words' bare meaning (denotation) and the form in which they appear (grammar). While individual words carry meaning, they do so much more clearly as they are placed in concert with other words. Often it is the nuance of intended meaning that is seen most clearly through the study of syntax in a passage.

For example, I am particularly taken with the ability of the Greek participle to provide tremendous insight into the "flavor" the author wishes to give to his writings; participle syntax is one of my favorite areas of study. For instance, there is great insight to be gained from noting the contrast of verbal forms found in Romans 5:1: "Therefore, having been justified by faith, we have peace with God through our Lord Jesus Christ." We are justified *as a past action* with the result that we enjoy, *as a present tense reality,* peace with God.[6] This kind of important information is often not present when reading a single English translation without reference either to multiple translations or to the original languages.

Form of Literature

Literary form is one aspect of hermeneutics most folks have heard mentioned, especially when their pastor begins a series through the parables of Jesus. We must recognize that the Bible

---

[6]For a fuller exegesis of this tremendous text, see my work *The God Who Justifies* (Bethany House, 2001), 236–41.

contains many different kinds of literature. Parables are not to be interpreted in the same way as an epistle; apocalyptic literature (Ezekiel, Daniel, Revelation) uses a different means of communicating meaning than does historical narrative (1 and 2 Samuel; 1 and 2 Kings). If you don't recognize such differences, you will not be hearing the author's intention. Entire sections of the Old Testament prophets are written in poetic form, as are the Psalms (a fact more clearly seen in modern translations that set the text off in poetic form, over against those translations that do not). Each of these literary forms brings certain "adjustments" to the rules of interpretation that must be allowed to have their say in the text's final interpretation.

Some people object to the recognition of various forms of literature, claiming that "we should always interpret the Bible literally." However, we are not interpreting an author of poetry *literally* if we ignore the specific medium he is using; that is, to insist upon a literal reading of, say, apocalyptic language is to ignore the original author's intentions and destroy the literality of our interpretation! *A literal interpretation is one that takes the intentions of the author seriously and, hence, will allow for different ways of speaking.*

For example, when Jesus utilizes symbolic language in John 6, He lays out His meaning first by defining His terms, saying that those who hunger and thirst are coming and believing in Him (v. 35). He defines the categories of hungering and thirsting as non-physical spiritual realities. Therefore, when He later speaks of eating His flesh and drinking His blood (vv. 53–58), He has already categorized such language; accordingly, the *literal* reading of His words is to read them *spiritually* (as v. 36 indicates) rather than *physically* (which would violate the definitions He Himself had established).

Immediate Context

Once background issues, grammatical issues, textual issues, and syntactical issues are addressed, we move to the immediate context—the sentence and paragraph in which we are working. The immediate context is the close-up; examining the entire passage, called *discourse analysis,* takes a wider view and sees the individual text as it stands in relationship to an entire argument or narrative. Each approach is important: Often the examination of the immediate context limits the possible meanings to a narrow range; then, with these possibilities in mind, the broad context determines which of these possibilities fits the overall narrative, the author's argument.

For example, sometimes there are two or even three possibilities that fit the grammar and syntax of a passage. However, when the passage is placed *within the writer's ordered argument* (such as exists in Paul's epistle to the Romans, where he has clear outline and linear argumentation), only one of these possible meanings fits with his argument. If the overall discourse is ignored, an improper interpretation of individual texts can be offered. This is one of the most oft-missed elements of correct exegesis, normally due to the presence of traditions in the reader's thinking. Popular, frequently memorized passages and verses (such as John 3:16) are most subject to this kind of error.

Scripture memorization is wonderful, but normally we memorize a short passage rather than an entire discourse. As such, we run the danger of picking the text apart, assigning a meaning to our favorite sections, and never truly considering if the way we have often heard the passage used is actually reflective of its sound exegesis. Interpreting a text so as to make the author contradict himself in his own teaching or presentation is a sure sign you have missed his intention. (Unless, of course, you begin with the assumption of "guilty until proven innocent," so that you assume the presence of contradiction in the text, which usually requires the modern interpreter to think himself wiser than the original author.)

Document Context

The next level of context is that of the entire document. As noted, Paul's epistle to the Romans has a clear outline, an argument pursued to its conclusion. John's first epistle plainly states that its purpose is to present Jesus as the Son of God so that by believing in His name the reader might have eternal life. Some documents, like Proverbs, can only provide an extremely loose

context. Others have a general theme, such as the Minor
Prophets (individually). When such a context exists, it must be
allowed to speak to the final conclusions regarding the interpretation of individual texts.

Author Context

The next level of context is that of the author. Consideration of how a particular author uses a term, for example, carries much more weight than referencing the use of that word
by someone else. Looking at a term as used by Luke or Paul or
John is more significant within the body of their writings than
it is across many contexts and authors.[7] As an illustration, note
that the parallels between Colossians and Ephesians carry more
weight, due to their having a common author, than would parallels posited between different authors. This is not to say there
is no value in comparing terms as used by different authors,
only that the context within an author's writings has a higher
value than any other.

Old Testament/New Testament Context

The last contextual categories encompass the Old and New
Testaments and, finally, the entire Bible itself. Obviously, as we
move further and further from the immediate context, we are
getting more and more into the realm of constructing an overall interpretation of the entirety of Scripture, precisely what
modern theological liberalism denies is truly possible. If you do
not believe that Scripture is, in its basic essence, *God speaking,*
you will not believe that you can transcend the level of the
author and have any true harmony or consistency. If Paul *does*
contradict Peter, or Isaiah *does* worship a different God than
Moses, then the construction of any consistent, harmonious
belief beyond the individual writings of the various authors is
simply a dream, a chimera, something that theologians have
pursued in vain. For many today, constructing a coherent message from Scripture is nigh unto tilting at windmills: a noble

---

[7]Many often assume that a word used in one context *must* carry the same meaning elsewhere, which is obviously untrue; further, it should be noted that an author himself can
use the same word in different ways. For instance, John uses the Greek term *kosmos*
("world") in more than a dozen distinct ways in the corpus of his writings.

task, but one grossly misinformed.

This is why we began with the truth of inerrancy and inspiration. Almost everyone agrees with the above insistence on examination of backgrounds and language and context, for this is what we have to do in examining any body of literature. But the Bible isn't just another piece of literature: If it is indeed the very words of God, and if (as we will argue in our next chapter) God has given it to the church for a specific purpose, then it follows that we do, in fact, have a solid basis upon which to believe we can *both* handle the text aright—honoring the intentions of the original authors, recognizing their differences in language, background, and even emphases—*and* believe that there is a divine consistency created by the supernatural work of the Spirit, who carried men along as they spoke from God in the production of Scripture, upon which the very foundations of the Christian faith can be safely and immovably based. This proposition leads us to a vastly important discussion.

THE REAL IMPORTANCE OF EXEGESIS

When it comes to the exegesis of Scripture, we are truly treading upon holy ground. While many view the interpretation of God's Word as nothing more special or important than the reading of any other ancient book, in reality the more appropriate attitude would be that which gave rise to the Jewish practice of washing hands when handling the scrolls of the Old Testament, for they believed that the Scriptures were so holy in and of themselves that they "made the hands unclean."[8] While we are not to become superstitious about the physical book called the Bible, the text of Scripture is, as we have seen, God-breathed. Hence, when we seek to engage that text on the level of understanding, *we are handling divine truth,* putting ourselves in a position to hear from God; this is remarkably different from merely seeking to comprehend the story of an ancient historian.

---

[8]Roger Beckwith, *The Old Testament Canon of the New Testament Church* (Eerdmans, 1986), 85.

This reality also sets believing exegesis apart from the common Bible study found in so many evangelical churches today. Remember when you were in school and you had to take a test on a book you were assigned to read? You studied and invested time in learning the background of the author, the context in which he lived and wrote, his purposes in writing, his audience, and the specifics of his text. You didn't simply come to class, pop open the book, read a few sentences, and say, "Well, I *feel* the author means . . ." (If you *did*, hopefully your teacher didn't give you an A.) Nevertheless, for some odd reason, this attitude is prevalent in Christian circles regarding the Bible. Rather than investing time in such allegedly non-spiritual pursuits as the study of backgrounds and contexts and languages and the like, many think it best just to seek a feeling or a sense about a passage. Whether this results in an interpretation that has anything at all to do with what the original author intended to convey isn't considered altogether important. Everyone seemingly has the right to express individual feelings about what he or she perceives the Bible is saying, as if these ideas necessarily reflect what God inspired in His Word. While we would never let anyone get away with treating *our* writings like this, we seem to think *God* is not bothered and, what is worse, that our conclusions are somehow authoritative in their representation of His Word.

If you have been wandering at all up to this point, focus now, because here is where the preceding pages about exegesis come into sharp focus.

*Sound exegesis is the only way of making sure we are allowing
God to speak rather than our speaking for God.*

Hear me well: We must always insist that God's Word be handled aright so that we honor Him, His authority, and His Word by hearing *Him,* for when we violate the rules of exegesis, we in essence force our words into His mouth. Poor or errant exegesis means we will not be hearing what God has said, but will, to some extent, be garbling the message with man's thoughts, man's traditions, or other earthly substitutes for the divine essence of God's truth.

Thus, *the ultimate reason for practicing sound exegesis is to be found in the commitment to allowing God to speak.* Again, without this we can claim nothing more than human authority for our preaching and teaching. What is it that allows us to believe that if before God we honestly seek in faith and obedience to hear only Him in His Word that we will actually be able to do so? In other words, what about those who say we're slaves to our presuppositions, bound to our traditions, and therefore *cannot* hear outside of a traditional interpretation, one determined by church history and the culture in which we live? Even in what would be considered conservative churches and movements, some have begun redefining *sola scriptura* in light of a belief that we cannot truly *know* what the Bible means outside of a certain set of inescapable preconditions created by church history and surrounding culture. As a result, these people believe that exegesis is secondary to other issues, including the study of various historical philosophies, the development of theology over time, medieval beliefs, and the traditions of all the major groups within "Christendom." Supposedly, without this kind of preliminary study, we can never really get to exegesis, and even then we will still only be able to come to an understanding of what the Word of God means *within our own cultural context.*

This viewpoint, though attractive to many, is fundamentally a denial of the perspicuity and inspiration of the Holy Scriptures. God surely did not intend the Word to remain solely in one culture, nor is there any reason to believe that written language cannot transcend cultural barriers. That we may have to make application of cultural aspects of the Bible does not mean the *message* is enslaved to cultural norms. Since the church was intended by God to go into all the world and teach (Matthew 28:19–20), it would hardly do to give the church an infallible rule and guide not up to the task. This is the whole reason for hermeneutics: to allow each generation, in whatever context, to have direct access—*not* access mediated by some growing and developing traditional authority that necessarily shuts off direct access to God's words—to God's truth *if they will but allow it to speak.* The rules of exegesis function as "tradition-detection devices," throwing up barriers to the insertion of foreign concepts into the text (*eisegesis*) and insuring that our conclusions are based upon what is actually found in the text (*exegesis*).

Anyone who asserts that the work of exegesis cannot rid us of our own tradition ignores the reality that the Scriptures had an inherent, inspired, constitutional meaning and intent *from the moment they were penned*. For example, if a person maintains that one must know and appreciate the influence of Thomas Aquinas (or certain medieval writers) to truly engage the text of Scripture, we are then forced to ask what the text meant *before* Aquinas produced his works and influenced the course of Christian thought. If the text carried that meaning then, why can we not ascertain it now? Knowing what Aquinas or Abelard or Anselm believed *is* vital for the study of the development of theology and church history, and there is no harm in such study *unless* we allow such a source to become a filter through which the inspired Word is forced to speak.

There is no question that our culture deeply influences our reading of the biblical text—or any other text for that matter. Even when we correctly draw a conclusion from the Scriptures, we may improperly insert it into a culturally derived paradigm. I am unaware of any conservative Bible scholar who has ever denied the existence of cultural influence in interpretation. Indeed, the entire reason for the strong emphasis upon *consistent* and *impartial* application of the rules of hermeneutics is based on the clear danger presented by such cultural intrusions into the process of interpretation. *This is the whole reason for carefully considering all of those factors and doing sound exegesis.* If you do not believe the original meaning is any longer accessible, why bother even referring to the text at all? Such a viewpoint inevitably leads to the embracing of some external authority, normally one of ecclesiastical origin and extraction, which then attempts to determine what is and what is not "tradition" and then speak for God by that means. Of course, the result is likewise the end of belief in Scripture's authority, for then the ultimate authority has clearly become the external source rather than the Word of God.

GLORIOUS CONSISTENCY

There is one other aspect to this topic that I desire to note before we must move on (or else turn the entire book into a discussion of exegesis). Over the past few decades of ministry in apologetics and in the study of God's Word, I have come to count as one of my most precious possessions the divinely ordained, divinely protected, divinely inspired *consistency* of the Word of God. Due to the nature of my work (apologetics, giving an answer for the faith), I am constantly faced with alleged contradictions in Scripture. I am always having to answer the "tough questions" from enemies of Christianity, within and without. This forces me into the text, into its language and its history, into its background and context. Through all of that work, and as a result of all those questions, I have come to see a divine consistency, a harmonious unity of the Scriptures that transcends any human ability to produce. Every human effort to overthrow this consistency fails and falters; as one of my professors reminded us years ago, you cannot define the word *truth* without using the word *consistency*. Consistency is the hallmark of truth, its outward sign and demonstration; that which is inconsistent is false by definition. So this inherent, all-pervasive consistency is one of the greatest discoveries I have made in working with the biblical text. Is it easy to see, lying merely on the surface? No, it can only truly be appreciated after we honestly struggle with the objections and attacks launched against God's Word. As when we work through these challenges, we will find God's truth able to stand up to the most difficult inquiries.

WHAT ABOUT THE SPIRIT?

We will dedicate a later dialogue to the discussion of biblical sufficiency and the claim that the Holy Spirit is giving new "revelations" to people on a daily basis. [9] To conclude our discussion here, we will answer the objection that such a focus upon the sound exegesis of Scripture in some fashion leaves the Holy Spirit out of the process. Isn't there a role for the Spirit in the

---

[9]See chapters 10 and 11.

study of that which He Himself produced? For many, the guidelines we have noted regarding sound hermeneutic practice seem sterile, scholarly, and anything but spiritual. However, are we really banishing the Spirit when we make a commitment to fully use our minds in honestly handling the Word?

First, I truly believe that *only* the Spirit of God motivates a person to make such a commitment from the start. It is God-honoring to say, "I do not wish to put words in God's mouth; I wish to hear Him clearly, so that I may be conformed to His truth, changed by the Word's ministry in my soul, and found obedient to His will." The natural man has no such desire.

Second, perseverance to work through the difficult issues so as to bring God's truth to God's people (i.e., the work of the elder who teaches and preaches) is likewise as spiritual an activity as one can possibly imagine. It is far easier to adopt the words of someone else, tell a series of heart-touching stories, and call it "good." Serious, intensive, long-term ministry of the Word in the context of the church takes a tremendous work of the Spirit, and when you see a man of God who has persevered in this work, do not praise him, but instead praise the One who has made him faithful.

Finally, I can honestly say that the deepest, most lasting spiritual experiences I've ever had have always been linked to Scripture. Working through the text of Isaiah 6 and the holiness of God . . . studying the truth of Christ's preeminence, eternality, and deity in Colossians 1 and 2 . . . peering in wonder through the veil of eternity at the relationship of the Father and the Son in Philippians 2:5–11 . . . pondering in amazement the Son's self-humiliation in giving Himself for me . . . all of these have brought an intimate experience of the Spirit's presence, not as He gave some new revelation, but as He enlightened that which He had already given and confirmed in my heart as truth and consistent with the rest of divine revelation. This is not the kind of spiritual ecstasy that will sell a million books, get you on TV, or launch you as a Christian media darling. But it is the kind of spiritual experience that lasts a lifetime.

CHAPTER 5

The Canon
of Scripture
Considered

The fact that many churches avoid uncomfortable topics, not only in the preaching of the Word but in Bible study as well, leads to the creation of blind spots in the theology of even the most devout Christians. These blind spots can then function as a door through which false teaching is introduced; hence the importance of doing as Paul said, preaching the "whole counsel of God" (Acts 20:27 ESV).

One such topic that makes many a Christian uncomfortable is the canon of Scripture. Why are there only so many books in the Bible? Could there be more? Less? What if new books were found? Who decided? On what basis? When? Can we really know?

The questions pile upon each other, and because most related resources stick to answering historical questions rather than delving into theological issues and ramifications, many believers have found themselves unprepared to deal with an attack upon scriptural sufficiency in a discussion of canon matters. To illustrate this, I begin with a "reversed" dialogue that, sadly, has frequently taken place with disastrous results. I include it only to impress upon us all the gravity of the subject to which we now turn. Since this approach is a Roman Catholic favorite, we'll consider a conversation between Gerry, a Catholic apologist, and Andy, a Protestant.

ANDY: Yes, I believe in *sola scriptura*. I believe the Bible is sufficient to give me the guidance I need to know God truly.

GERRY: But *sola scriptura* is a human invention, a tradition itself. Nowhere does the Bible teach it; in fact, the Bible contradicts it.

ANDY: The Bible contradicts *sola scriptura?*

GERRY: It certainly does. Not only does the Bible teach the necessity of sacred tradition, but the most glaring contradiction of *sola scriptura* deals with the canon itself. If you hold to *sola scriptura,* you simply cannot give any meaningful explanation of how the canon came to be.

ANDY: What do you mean? The *canon* of Scripture doesn't impact the *sufficiency* of Scripture.

GERRY: How could it not, Andy? How can you believe the Scriptures are sufficient as the sole rule of faith for the church if you don't even know what the Scriptures *are?* If the Scriptures depend upon an outside source[1] for their very existence, or at least for our knowledge of them, then how can they all of a sudden become sufficient once that outside source finally defines them? If they were dependent at one point in time,[2] why does that position of dependency change later on?[3]

ANDY: *God* inspired the Scriptures, Gerry. There was no outside source that made the Scriptures any *more* inspired.

GERRY: Of course not, but that isn't the issue, is it? How do *you* know, for example, that the gospel of Matthew is inspired but that the gospel of Thomas is not? How do you know Esther really belongs in the canon? Why do you reject Maccabees, when it was viewed as Scripture by early Christians?

---

[1]For example, a church, a council, a person.
[2]Before the canon was closed.
[3]After the council made its declaration.

Are you certain that Mark wrote the gospel of Mark? Does Revelation really belong?

ANDY: Well, there were various means the early church used . . .

GERRY: The early what?

ANDY: The early church—

GERRY: I thought that's what you said. So the *church* canonized Scripture?

ANDY: Well, yes, in a fashion. It wasn't like they *created* the canon, but they followed certain guidelines . . .

GERRY: Rules, perhaps?

ANDY: Well, yes—

GERRY: And where did they get these rules?

ANDY: It was just a means of making sure the writings that were accepted were genuine, related to an apostle of Christ—

GERRY: That's fine, but who says those issues determine the canon of Scripture? For instance, who made apostolic connection a test for canonicity? And what if the early church messed up? What then?

ANDY: I don't believe any errors were made . . . well, except when Rome added the apocryphal books. [4]

GERRY: You mean when Luther deleted them? We'll discuss that later, but you *do* admit that someone could mess up—in fact, in your opinion, someone *did* mess up regarding the deuterocanonicals, correct? [5] How do you know that didn't also happen in the third century or fourth century? [6] And if it did, what good is your *sola scriptura*?

See, Andy, without an infallible magisterium to give you an infallible Bible, you simply don't have the certitude you think you have. By rejecting the living voice of the church, the "pillar and support of the truth," [7] in reality you have bitten the hand that feeds you. You reject the very means God has used to give you the canon in an attempt to exalt those writings beyond the intention of God Himself!

---

[4]The Apocrypha is addressed later in this chapter.
[5]The apocryphal books are also known as the deuterocanonicals.
[6]When the canon was ecumenically addressed.
[7]1 Timothy 3:15.

ANDY: But Gerry, God never intended the church to be above the Scriptures.

GERRY: I never said the church is *above* the Scriptures. The Scriptures are part of the church's tradition, the written component. Once you overemphasize one aspect of tradition, the proper balance is lost, and this is what you have done. Teaching *sola scriptura* takes Scripture out of its correct relationship to the church; as a result, you can no longer explain how you even know what the Scriptures *contain*, let alone logically defend the idea of their supremacy in all things. Your position is left hanging in midair, indefensible. You must account for the canon, Andy, to even begin to defend *sola scriptura*. If the canon is a revelation from God, does it not of necessity exist outside of Scripture? How then can *sola scriptura*—Scripture *alone*—be true?

————

How would *you* respond to Gerry's arguments? For many, the issue of the canon is the Achilles heel of scriptural sufficiency; however, in reality, the above dialogue contains numerous faulty presuppositions and assumptions that must be challenged if a meaningful conversation about the canon is to take place. Unfortunately, those presuppositions and assumptions are almost never challenged, which forces the defender of scriptural sufficiency to defend concepts and ideas that are not only unnecessary but also *contradictory* to the truth of the position he holds. Before illustrating this in dialogue format, we need to consider the canon from a theological perspective.

THE CANON CONSIDERED

When we look to most of the modern, conservative discussions of the canon,[8] we learn much about the external aspects of the "canon process," like the historical considerations that can be discerned when we examine the writings of the early church or collate evidence from ancient manuscripts. We learn

————

[8]Such as the works of Bruce Metzger (*The Canon of the New Testament: Its Origin, Development, and Significance* [Oxford, 1987]) and F. F. Bruce (*The Canon of Scripture* [Inter-Varsity Press, 1988]).

about the importance that apostolic authority had to the early church in discerning between the genuine and the spurious, and how the text needed to speak authoritatively. We see clear evidence of the creation of collections of books, especially regarding the Gospels and Pauline epistles. We likewise see controversy regarding such books as Hebrews, 2 Peter, and Revelation. We learn that canonization, at least as experienced by the church in time, *is* a process, especially given that the New Testament books were not written and "published" at the same time or in the same place. Thus, some books were more known and more popular in particular geographical areas, becoming familiar to other sections of the church as years passed. Such would be expected given the culture and technology of the day and the speed at which communication took place. Books written in a particular area (or originally sent there) would have greater exposure than those unfamiliar to the local believers.

Going even further back we find a broad scope of unanimity regarding the Old Testament, especially among the writings of the Jews themselves.[9] As we will note in dialogue, the majority of Jewish writers did not embrace the apocryphal books, and the case against their canonicity is broad and weighty. Even so, there were also discussions concerning Esther, for example (which never uses the name of God), and the Song of Solomon.

History reveals to us that there *was* a process involved in the formation of the canon. No one claimed, at least at that time, that God had sent down a Golden Index from heaven so that there would be no need for discussion or discernment. Nor did anyone dream that an individual or an immediate circle of believers had the authority to canonize the Scriptures. It was recognized that *God had to inspire a writing before it could be canonical.* The nature of Scripture as revelation from God was recognized as the foundation of the concept of "canon."

History, though, can only reveal the *outworkings* of something divine in nature and intention. Historical inquiry can tell us, fragmentarily, *what* took place in particular areas, but it

---

[9]Roger Beckwith, *The Old Testament Canon of the New Testament Church* (Eerdmans, 1986), 85.

cannot make known *why* things happened as they did. For this, we must consider the only source that *can* tell us about Scripture's purpose and intention: Scripture itself.

What is the canon? The term itself does not specifically appear in the Bible, and we cannot come to Scripture and get a direct response to the question, "What is the canon, where does it come from, what is its relationship to Scripture, and how do we know it?" (at least not in the way we might seek such answers from an encyclopedia or an online manual). Thankfully, however, the Scriptures answer those questions in a deeper, more satisfying fashion. We simply need to frame our inquiries appropriately.

WHAT IS THE CANON?

The term *canon* originally referred to a stick by which a measurement was made. By extension it came to mean a rule or standard, and finally it was applied to an authoritative list of something, such as all the books written by a certain author or, in this case, the books of Scripture. However, if we think the biblical canon is nothing more than a fancy way of referring to the table of contents, we have missed the heart of the issue and will never arrive at a satisfactory answer to our questions.

I have become firmly convinced over years of study—including study of positive presentations by great theologians of the past and negative attacks upon biblical sufficiency from many different angles—that most discussions or debates over the canon start off on the wrong foot. A shallow, one-sided concept of the canon is usually allowed to determine the dialogue's outcome. If the canon is nothing more than the table of contents, then it is a purely human thing, known by men and hence subject to all the endless debates and arguments history presents as having already taken place in almost every generation. But what if the canon is more than that?

We need to start off by realizing we are talking about the canon of *Scripture.* As we have already seen, Scripture is *theopneustos,* God-breathed; to say we are talking about something unique is to master the art of understatement. Scripture does not simply drop down out of heaven like rain to be gathered up and organized by man. *The nature of Scripture determines the canon of Scripture;* that is, the canon must be defined in light of what Scripture is. If Scripture is (1) God-breathed and (2) given for the purposes revealed within its own revelation, then vitally important conclusions must be drawn from these two truths, conclusions that deeply impact our understanding of the canon and its function.

The reason I raise these issues is simple: I believe we must determine the divine view and purpose of the canon before we can have any basis upon which to discuss the human side of recognizing and understanding the canon. This may seem like a simplistic thought, but it seems often to have been left out in consideration of this subject: *Without the act of inspiration (revelation), there would be no canon.* So why think the canon of Scripture is to be determined and analyzed in the same way as the canon of the writings of, say, Plato, or Pliny the Younger? There are parallels, as we will see, but the fact that we are dealing with a book God intends to exist *in a particular form for a particular purpose* cannot be ignored.

The thesis I will seek to establish is this: The canon is an *artifact of revelation,* not an object of revelation itself. It is known infallibly to God by necessity and to man with a certainty directly related to God's purpose in giving the Word to the church. The canon exists because God has inspired *some* writings, not *all* writings. It is known to man in fulfillment of God's purpose in engaging in the action of inspiration so as to give to His people a lamp for their feet and a light for their path. The canon, then, has two aspects as we consider it in light of its relationship to God's overall purpose in giving the Scriptures. The first aspect, to which I will refer as canon[1], is the *divine* knowledge and understanding of the canon. The second aspect, which I will identify as canon[2], is the *human* knowledge and understanding of the canon (which has been the primary focus of debate down through the centuries). Hopefully, through this differentiation, we will be able to see through the fallacious arguments that far too often cloud the subject of the canon of Scripture.

THE CANON AS AN ARTIFACT OF REVELATION

Why does the canon exist? Perhaps this may seem far too obvious a question to even ask, but, having asked it, how many have ever considered it? Does the canon *need* to exist? Yes, it does, of necessity. Why? The answer helps us to understand one of the most common misconceptions concerning the canon.

When an author writes a book, a "canon" of his or her writings is *automatically* created as a result of the simple consideration that he or she has written at least one book, but has not written all books that have ever been written. Hence, a canon of a single book comes into existence at the completion of that first work. If the author continues writing, the canon changes with the completion of each project. It should be noted that even if the author does not write down a listing of his or her works, a canon exists nonetheless, which he or she knows infallibly. No one else can infallibly know this canon outside of the author's effort to communicate it to others, for only the author knows what he or she has truly written. Even those closest to the author may not know *with utter certainty* whether the author has used anyone else in the writing process or whether he or she has borrowed from someone else. Therefore, the originator of a book (or books) has an *infallible* knowledge of the canon of those works, while anyone else has a *mediated* knowledge, dependent upon both the honesty and integrity of the author and the author's desire to make that canon known to others.

When we apply these considerations to Scripture, we are able to see that canon[1] is the necessary result of God's freely chosen act of inspiration.[10] Once God's Spirit moved upon the very first author of Scripture, canon[1] came into existence. Before anyone else could possibly know what God had done (canon[2]),[11] God infallibly knew the current state and content of canon[1]. With each passing phase of His unfolding revelation in Scripture, canon[1] remained current and infallible, fully reflective (by necessity) of the ongoing work of enscripturation.

---

[10]Recall that canon[1] is the *divine* knowledge and understanding of the canon.
[11]Recall that canon[2] is the *human* knowledge and understanding of the canon.

This is why we should call the canon an *artifact* of revelation: It is not itself an object of revelation, but comes into existence as a by-product of the action itself. God inspires, and the canon expresses the limitation of that action.

Note something else as well: *Canon¹ exists whether or not canon² exists.* Canon¹ is necessary, while canon² is based solely upon God's desire to make known the extent of His act of revelation. Theoretically, God could keep canon¹ to Himself, leaving the world in utter darkness concerning what is and is not inspired. And even as God leads His people to gain knowledge of canon², *there can be times when the certain knowledge of canon² lags behind the actual content of canon¹.* The knowledge of canon² is dependent upon God's purposes at any given point in time, and if His intentions include using a human process in the creation of canon², that process may not result in a clear and widely known canon listing for some time *after* the giving of that revelation.

The nature of canon² in regard to inspiration is vital to properly understanding the historic canon process. Once we realize that *it is Scripture, not man's knowledge of the canon, that is inspired,* and that canon¹ exists perfectly in God's mind, we can see that the clarity and knowledge of canon² is dependent not upon human beings, councils, churches, or anything else in this world, but instead upon *God's purposes* in giving us the inspired Scriptures in the first place. Is a clear knowledge of the canon's extent important to the function of Scripture in the church? Yes. So does it not follow that God will both providentially preserve the Scriptures *and* lead His people to a functional, sufficient knowledge of the canon so as to fulfill His purpose in inspiring them? Indeed, will He not exercise just as much divine power in establishing and fulfilling His purpose for the Scriptures (their functioning as a guide to the church) as He has in inspiring them? These two actions are necessarily linked in fulfilling the one purpose of God.

As this issue forms a major portion of our understanding of the canon, we must provide a biblical foundation for the idea that God has a purpose in giving the Scriptures to the church and that He is intent on fulfilling that purpose.

GOD'S PROMISES REGARDING SCRIPTURE
AND THE CHURCH

We have already examined Paul's teaching on the nature of Scripture and noted its testimony to Scripture's ability to equip us:

All Scripture is breathed out by God and profitable for teaching, for reproof, for correction, and for training in righteousness, that the man of God may be competent, equipped for every good work. (2 Timothy 3:16–17 ESV)

God breathed out Scripture for many reasons, but the one included here is so that the man of God may be "competent" (or "thoroughly equipped") for every good work; specifically, so that he may teach, reprove, correct, and train—all "good works" of ministry within the body. In God's providence, the very form of the church, having elders in the position of teaching and admonishing and leading, requires it to have access to this God-breathed source of authority, the Scriptures. Therefore, the divine impetus to preserve and make known the Scriptures is equal to the divine impetus in forming and building the church itself—what good would it be to build a ship without a rudder? The Scriptures provide the direction, the guiding light, to the godly leaders of God's people in the body of Christ. Providing clear information relating to canon[2] is part of the fulfillment of God's purpose for the very structure of the church.

Long ago the prophet Isaiah spoke about God's redemption of Israel. Surely there was a direct fulfillment of these words in his day, but it is clear in reading chapter 55 that the prophetic voice soars far beyond the immediate context of Isaiah's ministry. Listen to his words:

For as the heavens are higher than the earth,
So are My ways higher than your ways
And My thoughts than your thoughts.
For as the rain and the snow come down from heaven,
And do not return there without watering the earth
And making it bear and sprout,

And furnishing seed to the sower and bread to the eater;
So will My word be which goes forth from My mouth;
It will not return to Me empty,
Without accomplishing what I desire,
And without succeeding in the matter for which I sent it.
(vv. 9–11)

The promise of the effectual ministry of God's Word has, as its *immediate* application, reference to the prophetic word He gave through Isaiah concerning the deliverance of Israel. But the entire passage goes far beyond this context: The assurance Israel has of God's favor is based upon overarching themes, such as God's transcendence over creation and the absolute certainty of His Word. What is true of His "Word" as prophecy is likewise true of His "Word" in the wider category of Scripture. The Lord Jesus may well have been reflecting this general theme of Scripture's infallible power in fulfilling God's purpose and intention when He said to the Jews, "The Scripture cannot be broken" (John 10:35). He did not have to prove His point: It was a given. It is part of the very nature of God's Word to be unfailing, utterly trustworthy and reliable, always successful in accomplishing His purpose. Scripture, therefore, has a *purpose* that God will ensure it fulfills.

There are multiple reasons why God has given us Scripture, but one that is vitally important to the canon issue is noted by Paul:

> Whatever was written in earlier times was written for our instruction, so that through perseverance and the encouragement of the Scriptures we might have hope. (Romans 15:4)

It seems clear that those who were used by God in the writing of the Old Testament Scriptures did not do so with the primary thought in mind that their words, centuries down the road, would be a source of encouragement for Jews and Gentiles, united in the one body of Christ. But God's intent in the writing of Scripture is here expressed in plain words: The immediate purposes of the prophetic ministry, while used as means to bring the Scriptures into existence, are subservient to

God's overarching purpose, which is providing the body with its chief means of encouragement and guidance. What was written "before" or in "earlier times" was written not just for those who lived then—a greater purpose was in sight, as it was written "for our instruction." The term *instruction* here is the same term Paul uses in his directive to Timothy:

> Pay close attention to yourself and to your *teaching;* persevere in these things, for as you do this you will ensure salvation both for yourself and for those who hear you. (1 Timothy 4:16, emphasis added)

"Teaching," sometimes translated "doctrine," appears often in Paul's epistles to Timothy and is one of the four terms used in 2 Timothy 3:16 regarding the duties of the church leader that by the God-breathed Scriptures he is enabled to perform.[12] Hence, Paul explicitly teaches that the divine purpose in the writing of Scripture included the future instruction and teaching of believers in the church, resulting in their being encouraged so that they might have hope. Indeed, he says the same thing to the Corinthians:

> Now these things happened to them as an example, and they were written for our instruction, upon whom the ends of the ages have come. (1 Corinthians 10:11)

Here a different term for *instruction* is used, one that refers to an inclusion of warning, even rebuke. Again, the overarching purpose for giving Scripture is seen: God orchestrated the events so that their actions would provide an example from which we could learn. If those events were not enscripturated, we would not benefit from the example; so the purpose of Scripture determines the clarity with which it is given and the effort God puts forth to make sure we are able to possess (preservation) *and* know its content (canonization).

THE CANON AND THE CHURCH

Considering the relationship between the canon and the church, so few discussions of this issue start with any clear idea

---

[12]See also 1 Timothy 1:10; 4:13, 16; 5:17; 6:3; 2 Timothy 4:3; Titus 2:1, 7.

of the *nature* of the canon that many people subsequently oper-
ate upon certain false assumptions about it, leading to tremendous (and unnecessary) confusion. For example, if we do not
differentiate between canon[1] and canon[2] and assume that the
canon itself is the object of revelation as to its content, myriad
questions arise regarding this final, cut-off bit of "revelation."
Who received it? When was it given? Will more be coming? If
an apostle did not give it, how is it verifiable? And if we do not
view it as revelatory but as a fragment of "tradition," is it apostolic in origin? If so, was John (the last of the apostles, according to tradition) entrusted with the collation of the entire
Bible? Where do we find evidence of this in the historical documents? To whom did he entrust the canon? Why does it take
so long for this apostolic tradition to become known?

The recognition of the canon's actual nature likewise helps
us to appreciate fully the church's role without falling into
error on the subject; that is, one can confess the *instrumental
nature* of the church in being used of God as the primary
means of establishing canon[2] without violating Scripture's
teaching by investing in the *church* some notion of infallibility.
Many have argued that unless the canon[13] is defined "infallibly" by the church, then no one can truly know it, but we are
now in a position to recognize the error of such an assertion.
*The foundation of the certainty of our knowledge of the canon is based
upon God's purposes in giving Scripture, not upon the alleged authority of any ecclesiastical body.* God did use the church, the gathered
body (not later ecclesiastical developments regarding unbiblical structures and positions), as a *means* to establish widespread
knowledge of canon[2] *so that* Scripture will function as He has
decreed it to function. But to locate the certainty of the canon
in an ecclesiastical body is to miss the glory of the truth: The
canon's certainty is found in its author and in the outworking
of His purposes for Scripture itself! God's sovereign power
stands behind the revealing of canon[2] over time through the
work of His Spirit, which led to a nearly unanimous view of the
New Testament canon.[14]

---

[13]Without identifying *which* aspect is being discussed—canon[1] or canon[2].
[14]See the argument of Roger Nicole, "The Canon of the New Testament" in *Journal of the
Evangelical Theological Society*, 40:2 (June 1997): 204.

Now, human unanimity is no more the sign of this work's completion than human unanimity on the nature of the gospel was necessary for Paul to say that its truth had been made known in his day (Galatians 2:5, 14), or for Jude to speak of the "once for all delivered to the saints" faith (Jude 3). Paul and Jude both knew there were many who disagreed with the truth of the gospel, but this did not diminish the reality of the revelation of its truth. Likewise, pointing to canonical disagreements does not mean God has not accomplished His will in leading His people to a sufficient knowledge of canon[2]. Indeed, with reference to the New Testament, there is hardly any meaningful disagreement to be noted,[15] and as we will see, the disagreements on the Old Testament are not nearly as difficult to sort out as some would have us believe.

It should be emphasized that the *primary focus* of God's work in giving a knowledge of canon[2] has been the *people of God*. This makes perfect sense: It is they who, indwelt by the Holy Spirit, hunger and thirst for the Word of God, and they are the ones to whom the Scriptures were given for instruction and encouragement. In other words, the Spirit's work was "bottom up," not "top down"; it was God's people, gathered in worship and service to Christ, who passively received, from the hand of God by His Spirit, a functioning, sufficient knowledge of the canon. This led then to the outward, official recognition by the ecclesiastical structures of later church history. But the order is important to observe: When Athanasius wrote his 39th Festal Letter (A.D. 367), listing the same New Testament canon we use today and the Protestant Old Testament canon,[16] he was neither "creating" the canon nor "originating" the knowledge of it. He was reflecting, as a bishop, the work the Spirit had

---

[15]Obviously, many disagree with this statement, pointing to isolated statements all over the historical record as evidence. But it is precisely the scattered nature of these statements, and the fact that they never reflect a consensus of believers over any period of time or great distance, that substantiates my claim. It is good that there were those who questioned canonical works, especially when they first appeared in a particular area; *de facto*, open arms and untested acceptance of *any* "scripture" indicates a lack of discernment. The reception of some works *in the particular area of their original authorship* is likewise understandable, even if such works never gained currency outside of the geographical area of their origination.

[16]The only exception being Greek additions to canonical books found in the apocrypha.

already been accomplishing for nearly three centuries. Augustine expressed it thus:

> Let us treat scripture like scripture, like God speaking; don't . . . look there for man going wrong. It is not for nothing, you see, that the canon has been established for the Church. This is the function of the Holy Spirit. So if anybody reads my book, let him pass judgment on me. If I have said something reasonable, let him follow, not me, but reason itself; if I've proved it by the clearest divine testimony, let him follow, not me, but the divine scripture.[17]

The Holy Spirit provides the canon for the church; the church does not establish the canon by her own authority. Does the Spirit do this by new divine revelation? No, by His work among the people of God, in whom He dwells.

The result of these considerations is clear: Those who think we must invest a divine attribute of infallibility in the church so as to gain a functional canon have misunderstood the canon's nature as an artifact of revelation (canon[1]), the nature of man's knowledge of that work of revelation (canon[2]), the purpose and promise of God in reference to the giving of Scripture, and the nature of the church itself. At the same time, those who despair of certainty regarding the canon will find in these considerations reason for rejoicing, because the true foundation for confidence in the canon of Scripture is found in God's sovereign power to fulfill His own purposes (Psalm 135:6), and it is His purpose for Scripture to function in the church as a means of instruction, admonishment, and encouragement.

AN OPEN CANON?

Another important theological and apologetic consideration: Is the canon of Scripture open or closed? That is, might there someday be eighty books of Scripture, or a hundred, rather than sixty-six, or is the canon a closed entity, without possibility of addition?

---

[17]Augustine, Sermon 162c, *The Works of Saint Augustine: A Translation for the 21st Century,* trans., Edmund Hill, ed., John Rotelle (New City Press, 1997), III.11.176.

For some this question is merely a fun theological brain-teaser, something along the lines of "What if we found a lost epistle of Paul—would it be included in the Bible?" But for others it is far more than mere speculation: Mormonism believes in an open canon, the possibility of "latter-day revelation," and on that basis seeks to have the *Book of Mormon* and its other scriptures accepted within the canon. Speculation on this topic has enjoyed varying popularity with each generation down through the course of history.

But the issue of the canon's extent is clearly addressed by the considerations we have already examined. The entire idea of "lost scripture" requires us to believe that God would go through the work of inspiring His Word so as to provide for His church guidance and instruction and encouragement; but then, having inspired His Word, be shown incapable of protecting and preserving it and leading His church to recognize it for what it is. Arguing that God might wish to give more Scripture at a later point is one thing; charging God with delinquency of duty in light of His own stated purposes for the giving of Scripture is simply without any foundation in His truth as taught in the Bible. From a biblical perspective of God's sovereignty, the idea of "lost scripture" is an unambiguously self-refuting concept.

But what of the concept of "*continuing* revelation" in the form of new Scripture from God? The idea is popular not only among those who wish to include their "revelations" in the canon, but also among those who use "the Lord spoke and said to me" formula with regularity. We will address the latter concept elsewhere,[18] but what response can be offered to those who believe the canon itself remains open? The previous considerations are again relevant. One would have to hold a view of the church that allows for a complete revision of its purpose beyond that envisioned by the apostles of the Lord Jesus Christ. In fact, the revelation of God in Christ, at best, would have to be considered either partial or liable to further future elaboration. This is *not* what the apostles themselves taught. Note these words from Hebrews:

---

[18]See chapter 10.

God, after He spoke long ago to the fathers in the prophets in many portions and in many ways, in these last days has spoken to us in His Son, whom He appointed heir of all things, through whom also He made the world. (1:1–2)

There are two modes of revelation noted by the writer: that which was spoken "long ago" and that which has been spoken "in these last days." The old way was directed to "the fathers" and utilized the prophetic writings. That which has been given in the last days is "in His Son." The rest of the book in numerous ways demonstrates the supremacy of Christ over everything that was part of the "old way"; therefore, envisioning a time when the revelation made in Him will be supplemented or even eclipsed by some new revelation would require us to abandon belief in the finality and supremacy of the revelation of God in Christ. The "last days" would have to be modified to allow for some later period when revelation would again need to be provided, as if the original provision was insufficient for the church. This, of course, is the fundamental drive behind all such allegedly "new revelation," which would likewise require a redefinition of the church and its mission (also common among those seeking to add to the canon). By contrast, if one accepts the New Testament's own teaching concerning both the perpetuity and nature of the church and the finality of God's revelation in Christ, the concept is seen to be inconsistent with the canon as it exists.

Someone conceivably could suggest that changing times have made it necessary for God to give new revelation, but the Scriptures teach that God is eternal and has infallible knowledge of the future; He surely knew every situation the church would face when He inspired the Scriptures long ago. Are we to believe that He is incapable of giving a revelation that would be sufficient throughout the church age? The Spirit of God *is* able to apply the principles and truths of the inspired Word to our hearts just as He did in past generations, and while our technology may be far ahead of our ancestors', our hearts and minds are the same. We remain the fallen sons and daughters of Adam, with the same needs and desires.

BUT WHAT OF THE APOCRYPHA?

A number of excellent works exist on the Old Testament canon, specifically regarding the question of the apocryphal books (deuterocanonicals).[19] Rather than repeat what elsewhere has already been written in full, we will provide a dialogue leading finally into a reprise of the canon issue with which we began this chapter. Gerry also will return, but this time he will be speaking with Joshua. We join their conversation midstream:

JOSHUA: I am *not* saying I embrace everything Martin Luther ever said or every concept he ever enunciated. I embrace the good and reject the bad, just like I do with all those who wrote after the apostles.

GERRY: But the man was simply beyond humility. He deleted books from the Old Testament—

JOSHUA: The deuterocanonicals, as you call them?

GERRY: Yes, books that had been used by believers for centuries. He rejected them because they taught things he did not accept, such as purgatory.

JOSHUA: Ah, the passage about idolatrous Jews who fell under God's judgment.[20] I never have figured out how that has any relevance to the notion of purgatory, outside of the statement that some Jews prayed for them after they died. You don't think praying for men who died as idolators is relevant to the Catholic doctrine of purgatory, do you? Is idolatry a venial sin?[21] Surely not.

GERRY: The point is, it contained a teaching unfriendly to Protestant belief.

JOSHUA: The Apocrypha contains all sorts of teachings and statements that are unfriendly to any belief in *truth itself.* There are so many internal indications that not even its own authors recognized they were writing in a period between

---

[19]See in particular Roger Beckwith, *The Old Testament Canon of the New Testament Church* (Eerdmans, 1986); David King and William Webster, *Holy Scripture: The Ground and Pillar of Our Faith,* Vol. II (Christian Resources, Inc., 2001), 301–434.

[20]2 Maccabees 12:39–45.

[21]For definition/explanation regarding "mortal" and "venial" sin, see my book *The Roman Catholic Controversy* (Bethany House, 1996), 126.

when the prophets of old had prophesied and when a new day was coming. One of the most popular of those works, 1 Maccabees, often notes that prophecy had ended during the time in which it was written.[22] Given that the New Testament writers constantly make reference to the Scriptures under the rubric "the law and the prophets," how could a writing specifically indicating that prophets were *not* in the land be called Scripture? Our misgivings are further increased by such lines as this: "I also will here make an end of my narration. Which if I have done well, and as it becometh the history, it is what I desired: but if not so perfectly, it must be pardoned me."[23] Some of the other writers *should* have been as self-effacing, like the author of Judith, who starts his book by saying that Nebuchadnezzar was king of the Assyrians and ruled in Nineveh. I'm sure this would have been of interest to Nebuchadnezzar, who was king of the Babylonians and ruled in Babylon.

GERRY: That last citation is simply proof that the writer is indicating through obvious error that his book is a parable.

JOSHUA: An imaginative defense, I confess, but one without parallel in the canonical Scriptures, as you would have to admit. Nowhere does the text itself indicate this meaning. The same verse speaks of Arphaxad, ruler of the Medes—is this likewise supposed to point us to some kind of parable? No, this is wishful thinking, and there are many such theological, historical, and grammatical issues in these books. There is a reason why the Jews did not embrace these books as canonical.

GERRY: The point I made is that *Luther* rejected those books.

JOSHUA: Yes, he did, *along with* the Jews, to whom the oracles of God were entrusted,[24] as well as Melito of Sardis, Origen, Athanasius, Jerome,[25] and, ironically, Pope Gregory the Great . . . plus more than fifty ecclesiastical writers up to the time of the Reformation, by at least one count.[26]

---

[22]1 Maccabees 4:46; 9:27; 14:41.
[23]2 Maccabees 15:38–39.
[24]See Romans 3:2.
[25]Jerome produced the Vulgate, the Latin translation of the Scriptures.
[26]See the discussion in William Webster, *The Old Testament Canon and the Apocrypha* (Christian Resources, 2002), 53–83.

GERRY: Wait a minute. Jerome translated the deuterocanonicals.

JOSHUA: Of course he did. That doesn't mean he considered them canonical, and, in fact, he didn't. He viewed them as secondary works, useful and beneficial, but not for the establishment of doctrine. There really isn't any question about this. Consider the words of Cardinal Cajetan, the prelate who interviewed Luther early in the Reformation—and a Roman Catholic if there ever was one—writing prior to the Council of Trent:

> Here we close our commentaries on the historical books of the Old Testament. For the rest (that is, Judith, Tobit, and the books of Maccabees) are counted by St. Jerome out of the canonical books, and are placed among the Apocrypha, along with Wisdom and Ecclesiasticus, as is plain from the Prologus Galeatus. Nor be thou disturbed, like a raw scholar, if thou shouldest find anywhere, either in the sacred councils or the sacred doctors, these books reckoned canonical. For the words as well as of councils and of doctors are to be reduced to the correction of Jerome. Now, according to his judgment, in the epistle to the bishops Chromatius and Heliodorus, these books (and any other like books in the canon of the Bible) are not canonical, that is, not in the nature of a rule for confirming matters of faith. Yet, they may be called canonical, that is, in the nature of a rule for the edification of the faithful, as being received and authorized in the canon of the Bible for that purpose. By the help of this distinction thou mayest see thy way clear through that which Augustine says, and what is written in the provincial council of Carthage.[27]

GERRY: Cajetan was a private theologian.[28] But what do you mean about Gregory the Great?

JOSHUA: Gregory cited an incident from 1 Maccabees 6:46 and specifically said Maccabees was "not canonical."[29] And the *New Catholic Encyclopedia* pointedly confirms his rejection of the canonicity of Maccabees.[30]

---

[27] *Commentary on All the Authentic Historical Books of the Old Testament,* cited in William Whitaker, *A Disputation on Holy Scripture* (Cambridge University Press, 1849), 48.
[28] An allegation meaning that he wasn't speaking for the entire Roman Catholic Church.
[29] *Morals on the Book of Job,* Vol. 11, parts III and IV, Book XIX.34.
[30] *New Catholic Encyclopedia* (McGraw-Hill, 1967, rev. ed. 2003), II:390.

GERRY: He too must have been speaking as a private theologian at that point.

JOSHUA: Actually, Gregory finished writing that book while he was pope, which makes one wonder how he would not be aware of the "apostolic tradition" defining the canon. Be that as it may, that particular book is terrible, an amazing example of allegorical interpretation and *foundational* to the development of the doctrine of purgatory in the Middle Ages. Ironic, isn't it?

GERRY: No dogma is dependent upon a single person.

JOSHUA: I'm sure that's true, but Gregory's contribution to what was eventually made dogma is acknowledged by all. Anyway, even Cardinal Ximenes, in his introduction to the first printed edition of the Greek New Testament, presented the same rejection of full canonical status to the apocrypha that Cardinal Cajetan documented, and yet Pope Leo X still approved the publication of the work. It is simply beyond controversy that at the beginning of the Reformation, the dogmatic stance taken at the Council of Trent was *not* the view of the best read and scholarly Roman Catholic leaders of the communion.[31]

GERRY: Even if there was such a confusion then, those books long before had been declared canonical, at Hippo and at Carthage. If you accept the New Testament canon created by those councils, then you should accept what they said about the Old Testament as well.

JOSHUA: Gerry, neither council had any concept of "creating" a church-wide canon by its deliberations. Both were local, provincial councils, not ecumenical councils, even by your own definition. Also, both represented the views of a single theologian—Augustine—who considered those books canonical primarily because they appeared in the Greek Septuagint.[32] Unlike Jerome, Augustine could not read Hebrew—he was not overly skilled in Greek either—and he mistakenly thought the Jews had likewise embraced those

---

[31]See William Webster's useful discussion in *Holy Scripture*, 2:359–434.
[32]The Septuagint (LXX) is a Greek translation of the Old Testament.

books as canonical.[33] In any case, the conflict between
Augustine and Jerome over the issue is well known, and I
do not believe you want to make reference to Carthage and
Hippo at this point: their canons differ from Trent's.

GERRY: What?

JOSHUA: Carthage used the Septuagint as its basis; the Septuagint contained 1 and 2 Esdras, which, in that version, com-
prised the extra-canonical additions to Ezra and Nehemiah
(1 Esdras) along with the canonical Jewish version of Ezra
and Nehemiah combined into one book (2 Esdras). But
Trent used the Vulgate; Jerome, knowing the Jewish canon,
had rejected those additions and thus separated Ezra and
Nehemiah. Hence, in Trent's canon—following the Vulgate—1 Esdras is Ezra, and 2 Esdras is Nehemiah. The *New
Catholic Encyclopedia* acknowledges these differences and
says that Trent "definitively removed it from the canon,"
"it" meaning the material found in the Septuagint version
of 1 Esdras.[34] The problem is seen when we recognize that
Carthage's canon, which included material *not* found in
Trent, was included in papal letters and decrees, including
those of Innocent I, Gelasius, and Hormisdas. How could
Trent infallibly declare to be *non*-canonical what popes a
thousand years earlier had accepted?

GERRY: Well, Joshua, this is why we have to start at the right
point. Trent's canon alone is dogmatic and infallible. Without an infallible church, Joshua, you simply can't know for
certain.

JOSHUA: So if I had followed the bishop of Rome's guidance
regarding the canon, I would have embraced non-inspired
documents for more than a thousand years until Trent
came along and corrected me?

GERRY: The difference is really not all that major—

JOSHUA: Gerry, the Septuagint version of 1 Esdras is longer
than the book of James.

[33]See Beckwith, *The Old Testament Canon of the New Testament Church*, 14.
[34]*New Catholic Encyclopedia*, II:396–97.

GERRY: Point taken, but you are still without an infallible determiner of your canon.

JOSHUA: Actually, you are left believing that Trent corrected popes in a fashion that would have led you into error for hundreds of years, and why do you believe this? Upon what basis do you trust the few prelates[35] who were actually in attendance when the final version of the decree on the canon passed at Trent?

GERRY: On the basis that I believe in the infallibility and indefectibility of the Church.

JOSHUA: Given what we just saw regarding the historical reality of your own "infallible" interpreter, I truly don't believe you have anything to offer as a meaningful example of an infallible arbiter of the canon. But let's lay aside Rome's own problems for a moment and see if you really have a point: *Why* do I need an infallible determiner of the canon?

GERRY: To avoid confusion so that you can know the Scriptures.

JOSHUA: So without this infallible pronouncement, I cannot know the Scriptures?

GERRY: Not really, no.

JOSHUA: Yet that infallible pronouncement was not provided until 1546? Dozens of generations of Christians muddled along without a clear and knowable Word from God?

GERRY: Those generations had the Church.

JOSHUA: Though we would disagree on the nature and identity of that church, yes, they definitely had the church. But are you seriously asserting that they did not believe the Word of God was clear and ultimately authoritative? Can you show me someone in the early church who basically said, "I would argue the Scriptures with you, but I really can't know them since I don't have an infallible canon; I'll just direct you to the bishop of Rome—he's infallible"?

---

[35]Robert Reymond indicates only fifty-three prelates, *none* distinguished for scholarship or learning, were present when the final draft was passed, the draft that has become "infallible" in Roman theology. In any case, Trent did not deign to offer a response to all of the factual information that stands opposed to their definition. See Robert Reymond, *The Reformation's Conflict With Rome* (Mentor Books, 2001), 22.

GERRY: No, I would not expect anyone to have spoken like that; some of those dogmas had not yet come to full development.

JOSHUA: Sounds to me like your demand for an infallible interpreter again founders on the rocks of history.

GERRY: I still do not comprehend how you can stand on *sola scriptura* if you cannot tell me with absolute certainty what books are in the canon and why others are not included.

JOSHUA: We look to different sources for our certainty, Gerry. You erroneously look to a human organization, albeit one you believe to be divinely guided, for your certainty. I look much higher, to the very plan and purpose of God.

GERRY: God's purpose is fulfilled in His Church.

JOSHUA: Of course, but that isn't relevant to the issue here; I am referring to God's purpose in giving the Scriptures *to* the church so that the church *can* fulfill her purposes. By limiting your appeal to a human institution, you end up with countless historical problems, and, since your final certainty rests there, that certainty is destroyed by the very historical facts we've discussed. But I appeal to a higher source, a higher authority, one that can accept and predict these historical elements but is not dependent upon a particular interpretation of them.

Gerry, that disagreement would exist is not a concern in light of God having chosen to use human instrumentality not only in the process itself but even in the proclamation of the gospel itself, that which brings Him the highest glory. God ordains both the ends *and* the means, but the means do not determine the certainty of the ends. That is, while we get the great privilege of being used of God in many aspects of His work, and while He has chosen to use the church *instrumentally,* the outcome of His sovereign purposes is not left hanging upon the *instruments* He uses.

———

Whatever the LORD pleases, He does,
in heaven and in earth, in the seas and in all deeps. (Psalm 135:6)
The counsel of the LORD stands forever,
the plans of His heart from generation to generation. (Psalm 33:11)

CHAPTER 6

Did Thomas
Write a
Gospel?

Y ou've seen it as you stand in line at the grocery store: One of those reputable literary journals with the picture of a space alien dressed as Elvis also has a great big headline that screams, "Bible Scholars Discover Jesus Lived in India!" or some other such bizarre claim. If you're brave enough to actually pick it up, or if the line is moving slowly anyway, you discover that these "scholars" are basing their conclusions on all sorts of books you've never heard of; you've never seen "The Gospel of Thomas" or "The Ascension of Isaiah" in *your* Bible . . . and when was "The Gospel of Mary" brought into the canon?

This element has been driven home with much greater force by the wild popularity of bestsellers like *The Da Vinci Code,* which spent half of 2003 at the top of the charts, selling millions of copies. You could see people sitting in restaurants, on trains, and in airports, devouring this work of fiction. Major media outlets like ABC-TV produced documentaries on the issues raised in the book, glibly informing their viewers that the early church had "suppressed" certain writings—the lost gospels—and that when those sources are consulted, a very different picture of Christ and His apostles and the entire Christian faith emerges. Such pop-level novels have tremendous impact upon those whom believers seek to evangelize, raising all sorts of new roadblocks to the proclamation of God's truth. Consider this typical conversation:

JOSHUA: That's why I believe it's so important to consider what God says about the way we live. Consider what the Bible says in Ephesians—

DAN: Wait, what the *Bible* says? Is that the old-style Bible, or the Bible that scholars have worked on since then?

JOSHUA: What do you mean?

DAN: As I understand it, the old Bible was made up by the church, and there were lots of important books left out, books that contained teachings no longer found in the original Bible.

JOSHUA: Have you read any of these books?

DAN: Well, not specifically, but I've seen scholars talk about what they contain and how they paint a very different picture than the books found in your Bible. So before you start quoting from that, how can you be sure what's in your Bible isn't missing important information that would alter what you believe?

———

How would you respond to Dan? Will you be prepared when this potential conversation-stopper comes in your direction?

THE APOSTOLIC WRITINGS

Despite the best attempts of those who seek to undercut the authority of God's Word, God's people from generation to generation maintain their confession that the Scriptures are God-breathed and therefore differ in their fundamental nature from any other human writing. Despite the nit-picking of skeptics and even the encroachment of unbelieving naturalism that pervades many theological seminaries, God's people hear the voice of their Lord in the writings that make up the Old and New Testaments.

The body of writings that make up the New Testament presents a consistent, harmonious worldview and message. From the four gospels through the epistles of Paul to the revelation given to John, a consistent, noncontradictory message of God's truth is provided for us. Again, that message is contained in different *types* of writing, and the authors used by the Spirit used different styles to communicate that body of truth. God used the concerns of each writer in the context of his own life and ministry to give us a fully orbed presentation of His truth. While different authors bring different life-experiences to their writings (Paul's experiences as an urbane Pharisee color his words, just as Peter's experiences as a Galilean fisherman influence his), their worldview is consistent: They all present to us one God, the Creator of all things, manifested as Father, Son, and Holy Spirit, one gospel centered in the cross of Christ, one sacrifice for sins, one Christian faith. Their outlook is thoroughly consistent with Judaism's emphasis upon monotheism, belief in one God. Nothing in their writings suggests a conscious break with the worship of the one true God who revealed Himself to Abraham, Isaac, and Jacob.

Why mention the continuity and consistency of the New Testament writings? Because when we look beyond the apostolic period—those important decades between the resurrection of Christ, the establishment of the church, and through the end of the last apostle's ministry [1]—we encounter precious few books that could be seriously considered for inclusion in the canon, and that for many reasons. The post-apostolic literature is as much of a grab bag of styles and beliefs as what's found in religious bookstores today. Some of these writings

---

[1] A great debate rages over when the last New Testament books were written. Some scholars go for a very early date, saying all New Testament books were written prior to the destruction of Jerusalem in A.D. 70. Major writers from a liberal position have posited much later dates for many books (also believing that books traditionally ascribed to, say, Paul, are actually the products of later generations). I would take the common view of generations of conservative scholars and see the end of the first century, and the ministry of an aged apostle John, as the far end of the time period during which the New Testament documents *en toto* were written (A.D. 95–98).

contain sound, orthodox teaching, while others demonstrate clearly that their authors had little knowledge of either the Old Testament or apostolic doctrine. While a few of these books were considered canonical by certain groups of believers, they never commended themselves to a wide audience of Christians.

Over the past centuries historical scholarship has dubbed the collection of works that circulated in the infant church immediately after the time of the apostles as the writings of the *apostolic fathers*. In general, these books include Clement's Epistle to the Corinthians (First Clement), The Didache, The Epistles of Ignatius, An Ancient Homily (Second Clement), The Epistle of Polycarp, The Martyrdom of Polycarp, The Epistle of Barnabas, The Shepherd of Hermas, and The Epistle to Diognetus. Some add a few smaller works to the collection, but this is a fairly standard listing.

It should be emphasized at this point that these are *not* the same kind of works as The Gospel of Thomas, about which we hear so much today. Though some rank low on the "meaningful and biblical content meter" (e.g., The Epistle of Barnabas and The Shepherd of Hermas), they are clearly written from a worldview that is at least *similar* to that of the New Testament. Unlike the "gnostic gospels" that we will examine later,[2] they do not come from a perspective that is *diametrically opposed* to the Christian faith as expressed by the apostolic writings in the New Testament. Though imperfect and impure (as any human writing would be), they do not show the same promotion of a dualistic view of the universe[3] that marks the second-century gnostic writings from a few generations later. The later gnostic writings are what make regular appearances in the supermarket checkout lines of modern America.

For now, a quick sampling of the above listed writings might

[2]See below, under "The Gospel of Thomas" (ff.).

[3]Dualism is the belief that what is spiritual is absolutely good, while what is physical (or fleshly) is inherently evil. This is a common element of gnostic belief, as we will soon see.

be helpful. [4] Further, knowledge of these texts helps to give a foundation upon which to evaluate the assertions of many in our day that the canon of the New Testament as we know it is somehow arbitrary and untrustworthy. Indeed, observing a few citations from these works reveals their pronounced contrast with the citations from the gnostic gospels that we'll see. All of these works are available in printed and electronic forms, rendering worthless the insinuation (found in many writings) that somehow these books have long been "suppressed" or "lost."

A SAMPLING OF THE APOSTOLIC FATHERS

CLEMENT'S EPISTLE TO THE CORINTHIANS

Clement's Epistle to the Corinthians (First Clement) is actually an anonymous work, written from the elders of the church in Rome to the congregation in Corinth regarding their having rebelled against the God-ordained leadership of their congregation. Most date it around the end of the first century. One of my favorite passages from Clement reads:

> Therefore, all these were glorified and magnified, not because of themselves, or through their own works, or for the righteous deeds they performed, but by His will. And we also, being called by His will in Christ Jesus, are not justified by means of ourselves, nor by our own wisdom or

---

[4]I pause here for a moment to lament the modern American Christian imbalance regarding church history. There seems to be almost no middle ground on the subject. The large portion of "evangelicals" view church history as extending back to the days of their parents, maybe their grandparents, but beyond that the history of the church is completely irrelevant to their own walk of faith. Few see themselves standing in that great long line of believers stretching back in time, and few believe they can learn anything from those who came before (an attitude that fits well with the hubris of the technological age); the result is the tragic truncation of God's faithfulness in the building of His church over the ages.

On the other end of the spectrum, however, are those who invest in the writings of any non-inspired writer (but especially those who wrote in the first centuries of the church) some kind of infallible insight into God's truth that makes their views or writings a lens through which Scripture itself is to be seen. The truth is: *Every generation must be tested by the same standard.* Every generation has "untaught and unstable" men (2 Peter 3:16) who put pen to paper, just as each generation has taught and stable men as well. But as our era has proven, the sound author is not always the most popular, so balance must be maintained. We must do with ancient writers as we do with modern ones: exercise discernment, take the good, let go of the bad, and in all things, be mindful that we will also need grace when we are evaluated by future generations.

understanding or godliness or works which we have done in holiness of heart; but by that faith through which the Almighty God has justified all those believing from the beginning. To whom be glory for ever and ever, amen. (XXXII)

Clement's letter is often misrepresented as showing some development of the concept of papal supremacy. It does not; at this point in time a single-bishop mode of church government had not yet developed in Rome. The mode we see in the New Testament, with a plurality of elders, remained in Rome until the middle of the second century.

THE DIDACHE

"The Didache," which means *The Teaching*, is a work that fits perfectly in the category of "moral instruction." Substantial debate exists over the document's dating; some place it in the first century, contemporaneous with Clement's epistle, while others suggest a date in the mid-to-late second century. Didache is not theologically advanced, but it sheds light on some of the church's ancient practices. Probably its most famous section reads:

But concerning baptism, thus shall ye baptize. Having first recited all these things, baptize {in the name of the Father and of the Son and of the Holy Spirit} in living (running) water. But if thou hast not living water, then baptize in other water; and if thou art not able in cold, then in warm. But if thou hast neither, then pour water on the head thrice in the name of the Father and of the Son and of the Holy Spirit. (7:1–5)

This passage is controversial because it is ancient testimony to baptism in the trinal formula of "Father, Son, and Holy Spirit." Those who deny the Trinity have a vested interest in denying the early date of Didache.

THE EPISTLES OF IGNATIUS

Seven genuine epistles (and a number of later pseudonymous letters) from Ignatius, the bishop of Antioch in Asia Minor, provide us with tremendous insight into the mind of a martyr. Ignatius probably died in A.D. 107–108, and his letters, though obviously not intended to provide a systematic exposition of the faith (none of these early writings were), give us important glimpses into early Christian beliefs. In contrast to Rome, Antioch had already developed the single-bishop model of church government, and, even more important, was dealing with key issues of Christian belief, including the deity of Christ.[5] Note these words from Ignatius to the church at Ephesus:

> There is one Physician who is possessed both of flesh and spirit; both made and not made; God existing in flesh; true life in death; both of Mary and of God; first passible and then impassible, even Jesus Christ our Lord. (VII)

More than half a dozen times Ignatius calls Jesus Christ "God"[6] long before any of the so-called gnostic gospels were penned. Phrases that echo the doctrine of the Trinity are found as well:

> Forasmuch as you are stones of a temple, which were prepared beforehand for a building of God the Father, being hoisted up to the heights through the engine of Jesus Christ, which is the Cross, and using for a rope the Holy Spirit. (v. 9)

Ignatius, then, is a remarkably important testimony to the early church's belief in many of the central doctrines of the Christian faith.

THE EPISTLE TO DIOGNETUS

The Epistle to Diognetus is an anonymous, incomplete record of one of the early church's most biblically oriented writings. The letter's theology contains solid evidence of New Testament influence, especially of the Pauline letters; its author is simply identified as "a disciple." Neither do we know when it

---

[5]A common point of attack for modern writers, including both Robert Funk, leader of the Jesus Seminar, and Dan Brown, author of *The Da Vinci Code*.
[6]For example, in XVIII: "For our God, Jesus the Christ, was . . . conceived in the womb of Mary."

was written, with proposed composition dates ranging from the time of Ignatius to the time of the Council of Nicea over two centuries later. In any case, the following citation is rich in New Covenant language, flowing clearly from a thoroughly Pauline understanding of the work of Christ.

This was not that He at all delighted in our sins, but that He simply endured them; nor that He approved the time of working iniquity which then was, but that He sought to form a mind conscious of righteousness, so that being convinced in that time of our unworthiness of attaining life through our own works, it should now, through the kindness of God, be vouchsafed to us; and having made it manifest that in ourselves we were unable to enter into the kingdom of God, we might through the power of God be made able. But when our wickedness had reached its height, and it had been clearly shown that its reward, punishment and death, was impending over us; and when the time had come which God had before appointed for manifesting His own kindness and power, how the one love of God, through exceeding regard for men, did not regard us with hatred, nor thrust us away, nor remember our iniquity against us, but showed great long-suffering, and bore with us, He Himself took on Him the burden of our iniquities, He gave His own Son as a ransom for us, the holy One for transgressors, the blameless One for the wicked, the righteous One for the unrighteous, the incorruptible One for the corruptible, the immortal One for them that are mortal. For what other thing was capable of covering our sins than His righteousness? By what other one was it possible that we, the wicked and ungodly, could be justified, than by the only Son of God?

O sweet exchange! O unsearchable operation! O benefits surpassing all expectation! that the wickedness of many should be hid in a single righteous One, and that the righteousness of One should justify many transgressors! Having therefore convinced us in the former time that our nature was unable to attain to life, and having now revealed the Savior who is able to save even those things which it was [formerly] impossible to save, by both these facts He desired to lead us to trust in His kindness, to esteem Him our Nourisher, Father, Teacher, Counselor, Healer, our Wisdom, Light, Honor, Glory, Power, and Life. (IX)

Much more could be said, but this brief introduction will suffice as a taste of the apostolic fathers. These are actually among the high points of those writings, some of which contain little theology or show little familiarity with major portions of the New Testament (which is to be expected, given the early date of their composition). Some even show a strong influence from non-biblical, primarily philosophical sources. Just as one finds a mixed bag of truth and error in the writings of our generation, so there were variations in the ancient setting as well. Let us now move on to the sources that are given such prominence today by those who seek to oppose the Christian faith.

GNOSTICISM: IS THERE A CURE?

For most people today, the term "gnostic" carries little meaning, sounding more like a physical condition than an entire religious worldview against which the apostles wrote and against which the Christian faith has fought for centuries. But since the vast majority of the sources upon which modern writers are basing their campaign to prove the Bible needs to be expanded (so as to include such works as The Gospel of Thomas) has been deeply influenced by gnosticism, we need an understanding of gnosticism's basic beliefs.

SECRET KNOWLEDGE AND DUALISM

Unlike the biblical worldview, which begins with a sovereign Creator, who has made all things, gnosticism overthrows the foundational assertions of Judeo-Christianity by asserting that the one true God is *not* the Creator of the physical realm. Why? Because gnosticism draws from a dualistic worldview, teaching that the spiritual realm is good and holy, while the physical realm is evil and profane. Since everything spiritual is good, how could the all-spiritual God create what is evil (the physical world)?

Gnostic dualism "solved" this problem by teaching that the one true God didn't create the physical realm; regarding its creation, gnosticism posits the concept of emanations, known as aeons, coming forth from the one true God. As each emanation in the series is a little further from the ideal God, they are a little less pure, a little less fully spiritual. Finally, down the line of aeons (the whole group being called the "pleroma"), comes a being that still has divine powers but is sufficiently removed from the original God that this being, called a *demiurge*, is able to create the physical world. Gnostics in the second century (around the same time as the writing of The Gospel of Thomas and other such works), who sought to find a way of melding Christianity and gnosticism (a movement illustrated best in the famous gnostic Marcion), identified this lesser, quasi-evil creator deity with Yahweh, the God of the Old Testament! They insisted that the Old Testament could not truly be Scripture for the Christian church, since it spoke of the Creator; they then limited what they would accept from the New Testament to that which they could fit into their system, a ploy strikingly similar to the workings of the contemporary Jesus Seminar.

Salvation in gnosticism involved taking in secret *gnosis* (knowledge) through various religious rites and ceremonies and initiations. This knowledge, it was believed, would allow a man to escape the confinement of his "flesh" and reach his true potential as a disembodied spirit. This is why the Greeks, who likewise embraced a dualistic worldview, responded so negatively to Paul's proclamation of the resurrection when he preached on Mars Hill in Athens (Acts 17:16ff., esp. v. 32). *Resurrection* means "that which died coming to life again"; they understood this as referring to the physical body rising from the grave, which is exactly what Paul meant. When he said this, they mocked him, for such would be the exact opposite of what they considered "true salvation." Paul was obviously not functioning on a dualistic basis, for the Judeo-Christian worldview affirms that creation, though now fallen, was *created* good by God.

And so we see that there is a fundamental conflict between the gnostic and Christian worldviews. They are *not* compatible, and any attempt to conjoin the two will result in the destruction of the unique, defining elements of the Christian faith. This was the reason believers fought so vociferously in writing and preaching against the rise of "Christian gnosticism," for such a description is an oxymoron, similar to "loving hater" or "faithful adulterer."

THE GOSPEL OF THOMAS

Thomas had nothing to do with the writing of this book; while it bears his name, its origin is from long after Thomas passed from this world. The author draws heavily from a gnostic worldview, while showing obvious reliance upon and familiarity with the canonical Gospels (Matthew, Mark, Luke, and John). This "gospel" is a second-century production, bearing marks of the beliefs expressed in what eventually became known as Valentinian gnosticism. [7] Again, it proceeds from a completely non-Christian (even anti-Christian) worldview, hence its value to those seeking to undermine the faith today—by promoting it, they are able to create the illusion of internal conflict and contradiction, thereby more easily sowing seeds of skepticism in the hearts of unbelievers and believers alike.

One of the most effective ways of revealing the true character of these works is allowing them to speak for themselves; the contrast with the Christian Scriptures is stark. Here are some examples to consider.

> Simon Peter said to them, "Make Mary leave us, for females don't deserve life."
>
> Jesus said, "Look, I will guide her to make her male, so that she too may become a living spirit resembling you males. For every female who makes herself male will enter the domain of Heaven." [8]

It is astonishingly ironic that Christianity's tremendous teaching regarding the value of women—their equality with men in standing before God and the honor given their role as

---

[7]A form of gnosticism popularized by Valentinus.
[8]Thomas 114:1–3, cited from Robert W. Funk and Roy W. Hoover, eds., *The Five Gospels: The Search for the Authentic Words of Jesus* (Macmillan, 1993).

mothers and wives—is ignored by so many who oppose the faith, yet those same people will embrace sources such as this that are so patently anti-woman in their viewpoint. Of course, this is helpful if one is seeking to *create* nascent-church disharmony; groups such as the Jesus Seminar have attempted to canonize The Gospel of Thomas by publishing it in their own translation of the Bible, characteristically titled *The Scholar's Version.*

> Jesus said, "Congratulations to those who are alone and chosen, for you will find the [Father's] domain. For you have come from it, and will return there again."
> Jesus said, "If they say to you, 'Where have you come from?' say to them, 'We have come from the light, from the place where the light came into being by itself, established [itself], and appeared in their image.'
> If they say to you, 'Is it you?' say, 'We are its children, and we are the chosen of the living Father.'
> If they ask you, 'What is the evidence of your Father in you?' say to them, 'It is motion and rest'" (49–50:1–3).

While The Gospel of Thomas borrows terminology and language from the canonical Gospels (especially John's use of "light" and "darkness"), it fills these terms with meanings utterly foreign to the biblical worldview.

> Jesus said, "I am the light that is over all things. I am all: from me all came forth, and to me all attained. Split a piece of wood; I am there. Lift up the stone, and you will find me there" (77:1–3).

Again the language of John is pressed into foreign service, promoting a form of pantheism opposed to the Christian belief that God's omnipresence (He is unlimited in time and space by His own creation) does not mean He is contained *within* His creation.

So is there any value to Thomas at all? Ironically, the fact that Thomas shows knowledge of major portions of the canonical Gospels, especially John, provides another external (and hostile) witness to the early dating of those gospels. It is often claimed that Thomas may provide us with a number of sayings of the Lord Jesus not found in the New Testament; while there could be an echo of an actual statement somewhere in that mass of gnostic myths, it would be next to impossible to determine whether it's truly a separate statement passed down outside the canonical Gospels or just a reworking of a statement from them. In any case, Thomas gives us insight into those who opposed the Christian faith by promoting a perversion of its most basic essence. Those who seek to canonize Thomas and place it alongside Matthew, Mark, Luke, and John do so at the expense of meaningful history.

THE GOSPEL OF MARY MAGDALENE

Until Dan Brown made a personal fortune promoting an entertaining but historically bankrupt fabric of mythology and conspiratorial thinking, very few had ever heard of The Gospel of Mary Magdalene. It is found in only a few manuscripts, and even then in fragmentary form; though its main source was discovered in the late nineteenth century, it did not appear in print until 1955. Magdalene bears clear signs of being derived from the same mythological ethos as Thomas:

> Then Mary stood up, greeted them all, and said to her brethren, "Do not weep and do not grieve nor be irresolute, for His grace will be entirely with you and will protect you. But rather, let us praise His greatness, for He has prepared us and made us into Men."
> When Mary said this, she turned their hearts to the Good, and they began to discuss the words of the Savior.
> Peter said to Mary, "Sister, we know that the Savior loved you more than the rest of woman. Tell us the words of the Savior which you remember which you know, but we do not, nor have we heard them." Mary answered and said, "What is hidden from you I will proclaim to you" (5:2–7). [9]

This particular section was highlighted in the ABC News special

---

[9]Text taken from The Gnostic Archive at *www.gnosis.org/library/marygosp.htm.*

on *The Da Vinci Code* and the theories propounded by Dan Brown. To some of those interviewed, the idea that Mary Magdalene is here shown great preference by the apostles suggests that "the church" found this "gospel" to be a threat to their male-dominated structure, which led to the wholesale destruction of the text. Of course, the less-than-thorough research put into the program failed to note that the church in those early centuries was under persecution and lacked the structure and coherence that would allow it to "suppress" much of anything at all. However, there is no doubt the church stood against this book and all other gnostic writings; just as the apostle John had warned about those who would deny that Jesus came in the flesh (1 John 4:1–3), so subsequent generations that followed the apostles' teaching likewise rejected the gnostic denial of Christ's incarnation, full deity, and physical resurrection. This was not due to some imagined dislike of female leaders in the church or any such thing: Gnosticism rips the heart out of the gospel because it removes from Christianity the truth about Jesus Christ, the foundation upon which the faith is built.

Just a few other citations from this gnostic production:

> Matter gave birth to a passion that has no equal, which proceeded from something contrary to nature. Then there arises a disturbance in its whole body. That is why I said to you, "Be of good courage, and if you are discouraged be encouraged in the presence of the different forms of nature" (4:30–31).

Here one can detect familiarity with New Testament language,[10] but it is still clearly placed in a non-Christian context. One last citation will close our brief introduction:

> "The first form is darkness, the second desire, the third ignorance, the fourth is the excitement of death, the fifth is the kingdom of the flesh, the sixth is the foolish wisdom of flesh, the seventh is the wrathful wisdom. These are the seven powers of wrath."
> They asked the soul, "Whence do you come, slayer of

---

[10]"Be of good courage" is found in Paul; e.g., 2 Corinthians 5:6, 8.

men, or where are you going, conqueror of space?"

The soul answered and said, "What binds me has been slain, and what turns me about has been overcome, and my desire has been ended, and ignorance has died" (8:19–22).

The connection to gnostic concepts of wisdom, knowledge, and the use of such items to gain supposed redemption from the flesh is plainly present in these passages. Mary Magdalene had nothing to do with such a work, of course, and this material represents nothing relevant to the Christian faith itself.

BETWEEN STOPS ON THE A-TRAIN

During the course of my ministry during the year, I spend a lot of time on Long Island. To get into the city, I take the Long Island Railroad, and often I will see people boarding with various books that catch my attention. What if Joshua, our redoubtable defender of truth, were on this train when Tina plops down in front of him, carrying a copy of *The Da Vinci Code*? He doesn't have much time—only a few stops left. Here's how it might go (assuming that any New Yorker would dare strike up a conversation on a train in the first place):

JOSHUA: I see you are reading Brown's work.

TINA: Yeah, it's great! Have you read it?

JOSHUA: Yeah. I started hearing a lot about it months ago. Sad that so many folks don't realize it's well-written fiction that doesn't represent serious historical research.

TINA: Oh, you don't think Jesus could have been married and had children?

JOSHUA: No, the legitimate historical sources—the ones that have a serious claim to validity and hence to our belief—preclude this, and the sources Brown weaves together are simply beyond credibility.

TINA: What about books like The Gospel of Mary Magdalene? I saw scholars on TV talking about it and about how the church suppressed her story.

JOSHUA: Well, actually, you saw authors who have written books promoting that view . . . promoting their books. You were not shown the other side. Ever considered that the primitive Christian church was hardly in a position to be chasing down copies of pseudepigraphal gospels penned by their enemies? I mean, remember that those people were hiding from Roman soldiers; if they got caught, they were being imprisoned and fed to lions? People in survival mode are hardly in a position to be worrying about destroying copies of disagreeable writings—agreed?

TINA: I hadn't thought about that before . . . but it's still fun to think about the possibility of Jesus being married.

JOSHUA: You know what's far more interesting? To consider the truth about Christ: how the very Son of God gave His life as a ransom for the sins of His people. Let me share with you how I came to know Him. . . .

CHAPTER 7

Allegations

of

Corruption

Another common attack upon the sufficiency of God's Word comes through allegations of textual corruption over time. The canon doctrine speaks to one aspect of this issue, that being the overall *content* of Scripture on the level of entire literary works (books). The issue of the actual *text* of Scripture goes beyond the canon and says (for example), "Since Paul's letter to the Romans has been given in God's providence to function as guide and guard of Christ's body, the church, we must address the *words* of Romans, the textual content. What does Romans *say?*" Here another attack is launched by those who insist we simply cannot know what was initially written since we lack the autographs, the original writings of apostles or prophets.

This denial of *sola scriptura* (how can Scripture be sufficient if we do not know what it *says?*) can be based on very different foundations and have very different goals. The atheist or skeptic may seek to overthrow the entirety of biblical revelation by alleging an inability to know the text of the originals. On the other hand, most of those who promote this particular argument do so from a religious foundation: They are either members of outside religions (e.g., Muslims) who use this argument to deny the validity of the Christian faith or they are members of groups that claim fidelity to Christianity yet seek to establish an extra-biblical source of authority. This is a common approach, for if you can instill doubt concerning the text itself, then you can seek to assert the authority of your leader/group/ organization and thereby subjugate Scripture to your group's interpretations, deletions, additions, traditions, etc.

Of course, one response to attacks upon the text of Scripture is to swing to the other side and embrace something like the King James Only movement, where a particular English *translation* is endowed with a supposedly supernatural character so that it becomes regarded as *the* standard text. I have fully addressed this subject elsewhere,[1] but note that such movements only undercut a meaningful and historically valid defense of the integrity of the biblical text. Just as Rome was in error to establish the Latin Vulgate as *the* primary text for the church in the face of the Reformation, so it is erroneous to establish any secondary text (i.e., a translation) as *the* text above and beyond the original.[2]

Knowing why we believe the Bible has been transmitted to us so as to fulfill God's purpose in having given it is vital for the modern Christian who must seek to proclaim God's truth in an increasingly anti-supernatural, anti-biblical context. Not only must we honor God by giving a reason for our faith (1 Peter 3:15), but such situations also often lead to opportunities to present the claims of Christ in the gospel.

The following dialogue is with Caleb, our LDS representative. Some of the more basic assertions regarding scriptural corruption could be voiced by others (atheists, for example), but Mormonism has put this assertion in the form of a doctrinal belief, as we will see. I learned long ago that there are essentially two groups in the world: those who bow to, obey, and love God's Word, and those who do not. The details may differ, but

[1]James White, *The King James Only Controversy* (Bethany House, 1995).
[2]This will take shape in the following dialogues.

the foundation remains the same.

CALEB: You can't possibly believe in the perfection of the Bible, Joshua—it so obviously has been changed over time!

JOSHUA: That certainly is not "obvious" to me, Caleb. To what do you refer?

CALEB: Well, you know that the *Book of Mormon* says many "plain and precious" truths have been removed from the Bible.

JOSHUA: Yes, in 1 Nephi.[3] I'm quite familiar with the claim, but I've never found any basis for it.

CALEB: But it seems so clear. I mean, it's not like they had copy machines back then. Surely things must have been deleted from the text, both inadvertently and purposefully.

JOSHUA: That's a more-than-common allegation, but when I ask for specifics, I'm normally disappointed. Tell me, Caleb, do you know how modern translations of the Bible—or the King James, for that matter—were translated?

CALEB: I remember one of our elders in Priesthood Meeting taking a passage from Matthew, one of the Beatitudes, and pointing out how a couple of words came from William Tyndale, a few from a German translation, a few from the Latin, etc. Sort of cobbled together.[4]

JOSHUA: That's not how it actually works, Caleb. Modern translations, and even the King James Version, are translated directly from the original languages of the Bible—Hebrew and a few chapters of Aramaic in the Old Testament, and the common Greek in the New Testament.

CALEB: But, Joshua, you don't have the originals!

JOSHUA: That's true, we do not. Truthfully, I fear even if we did, we would probably do what Israel did and fall into idolatrous worship of them. But it's a huge leap from "We do not possess the originals" to "We do not know what the

[3]1 Nephi 13:26–32.
[4]I am fully aware that LDS scholarship would not promote such an idea, but I sat in the Priesthood Meeting of the Glendale (Arizona) 6th Ward and listened to this *very* presentation made to the gathered people. Not a single objection was raised. Through nearly two decades of ministry to Mormons in Arizona and Utah, this understanding of how the Bible came to its present form has been the most commonly enunciated by the average LDS person.

originals said." Tell me, have you ever personally handled the original Declaration of Independence?

CALEB: No, but it still exists, doesn't it?

JOSHUA: Yes, it does; but since you've never seen it, you're trusting that the renderings you've seen are accurate. Answer this: If the original was somehow lost today, would we no longer know what it said?

CALEB: The Declaration has been copied repeatedly—of course we'd still know what it said.

JOSHUA: Exactly, and the same is true of the New Testament writings. We know what the originals said because we have what in scholarly circles is called a trustworthy and accurate *manuscript tradition.* We have a body of more than 5,300 manuscripts of the Greek New Testament, and about 20,000 manuscripts of translations thereof, such as Latin or Syriac. Now, not each one of those manuscripts contains the entirety of the New Testament—some contain very small portions, while others are complete texts. Many are from a relatively late time, say, the tenth or thirteenth centuries, while others take us back to the very beginnings of the faith, including some papyri that could date as early as A.D. 125.

CALEB: Yeah, I've heard about all this, but what does that have to do with anything? I mean, the manuscripts all read differently, don't they?

JOSHUA: That's just it, Caleb: The fact that we have such a wide and varied group of witnesses to the original text gives us complete confidence that the very claim you have made— specifically, that "many plain and precious" things have been removed from the Bible—is simply false. Let me explain why.

One of the terms used in scholarly writings about the New Testament text is *tenacity.* While we might think that means someone or something is tenacious—that they have a lot of "stick-to-itiveness"—in this case it's referring to the fact that once a scribe puts a particular reading into a manuscript, even if it's obviously in error, that reading will remain, even when the manuscript is copied.

CALEB: Which sort of makes my point, doesn't it?

JOSHUA: Well, think with me here for a minute. If the New Testament manuscripts from the original writing until the invention of the printing press[5] *do* demonstrate this characteristic of tenacity, whereby even copyist errors are passed on, what would that mean regarding the original readings themselves?

CALEB: If what you say is true, I guess that would mean they hang around too.

JOSHUA: Right. Now, don't get me wrong; in comparison with any other work of antiquity, the New Testament is by far the best attested. Its level of purity is unsurpassed, and the actual percentage of the text that requires in-depth analysis of variations in the handwritten manuscripts is amazingly small.

CALEB: But you admit it *has* been changed?

JOSHUA: No, "change" is a word that can be understood to refer to people sitting around editing or altering the text itself. I am referring to copyist mistakes, most of which were inadvertent errors of sight or, later on in the history of the text, hearing.[6] Other copyist errors included harmonization, where the scribe would make, say, a passage in Mark read like the parallel passage in Matthew, due either to his own memory of how the passage is "supposed" to go, or because he mistakenly thought each of the gospels should read like the others. In any case, such scribal errors are the most easily detected.

CALEB: Okay, I haven't heard that before, but then you admit that the Bible isn't inerrant?

JOSHUA: No, no, you're confusing two different issues. Inerrancy speaks to the perfection of the originals as they came from the pens of their authors. Those autographs (originals) were inspired and inerrant. Now, two thousand years later[7] the issue of how we know we have a reliable and accurate knowledge of what was in those inspired originals is the

---

[5]In the middle of the fifteenth century.
[6]Errors of hearing were possible when scribes used "scriptoriums," where one person read the text while a group of others copied what was read.
[7]At least as far as the New Testament period is concerned.

issue of *transmission* not *inerrancy*. It is important to differentiate between the two.

CALEB: You believe the Bible is inerrant, but copyists made errors?

JOSHUA: Yes. Remember, I spoke of the tenacity of the text and how that guarantees we still have all the original readings. Could I give you an example?

CALEB: Sure.

JOSHUA: Could you read 1 John 3:1 from your King James Version?

CALEB: Glad to. "Behold, what manner of love the Father hath bestowed upon us, that we should be called the sons of God: therefore the world knoweth us not, because it knew him not."

JOSHUA: Now compare a modern, mainly literal translation, the *New American Standard Bible:* "See how great a love the Father has bestowed on us, that we would be called children of God; and such we are. For this reason the world does not know us, because it did not know Him." Do you notice the main difference?

CALEB: Aside from the older versus the newer form of English, your translation contained an extra phrase "and such we are."

JOSHUA: Right—stay with me. When you examine the manuscripts of 1 John, you discover a common error of sight that explains the difference. Without getting into too much detail, the King James was based upon a small number of manuscripts representing the *later* form of the text, the standard Greek text of the twelfth through the fifteenth centuries. *Earlier* manuscripts contain the phrase "and such we are." So why do the later manuscripts not contain it? Because of the kind of visual error you and I have also made many times. Say you're copying quotes from a book and you run across a line like this:

When you examine a text, always watch for what comes next, or you will lose your way.

So you type the first phrase, which ends with the word

"text," and when your eyes go back to the original you're copying, instead of falling on "text," they find the later word, "next," which ends with the exact same three letters. So because of the similar endings,[8] the intervening phrase, "always watch for what comes" would be inadvertently deleted. Now, in this case, the copied sentence wouldn't make sense, which might result in the lost phrase being reinserted in the margin by a corrector or even by the scribe himself upon proofreading his work. In the case of 1 John 3:1, the resultant sentence did make sense: The Greek word for "we might be called" ends in -men;[9] the word for "we are" ends in the same three letters. So a small phrase, "and such we are," was unintentionally omitted from later manuscripts.

CALEB: How do you know it wasn't added in at some point, rather than having been in the original?

JOSHUA: Good question. First, there is an obvious reason why it could have fallen out without any malice on the part of the copyist, as I've just noted. Second, why would anyone want to delete a reference to believers in Jesus Christ being adopted into His family? Both of these issues refer to the *internal* evidence, which is evidence based upon the reading of the text itself. But then we can also look at the *external* evidence, that of the manuscripts themselves. In this case, the majority of the *earliest* texts, as well as the earliest translations into other languages, contain the phrase "and such we are." The majority of those do not give evidence of interrelationship; that is, of being derived from the same family of later manuscripts. Therefore, the combination gives us firm reason for reading the text with the phrase "and such we are."

But remember, Caleb, the issue of tenacity. There are only two readings for this phrase, and one of them is original. Nothing has been "lost." And please realize, most of the New Testament text does not even present *this* level of

---

[8]Hence the technical name of this common error, *homoeoteleuton,* meaning "similar endings."
[9]Greek "mu epsilon nu."

variation. For example, 1 John 3:3 presents no meaningful variants—two thousand years, hundreds of manuscripts, and no variation at all.

CALEB: I can see your point as far as 1 John 3:1 goes. I can even see that since all of these manuscripts were written by hand, there will be unintentional variations and that sort of thing. But if you say the Bible is perfect, how do you square that with the existence of this kind of variation?

JOSHUA: You are not the only one to wonder about this, I assure you. But let me make two very important points.

First, I think the example of Jesus and the apostles is significant here. The New Testament writers constantly cited from a Greek *translation* of the Old Testament, commonly called the Septuagint.[10] In fact, in some places they quote the Greek version even when it differs from the Hebrew.[11] Why mention this? If the Lord Jesus Himself and His disciples did not think the existence of such minor differences meant the Word had been corrupted, we shouldn't either. Jesus said the Scripture "cannot be broken,"[12] and unless we somehow insist that the Lord was ignorant in this regard, we need to follow His example.

Second—and this is vital—consider that minor textual variations are merely the by-product of the very means the Lord chose to preserve His Word. And this is where I really have to point out the error of the LDS claim of wholesale editing and corruption of the Bible. Think about it: Paul writes his letter to the Ephesians. It is transported to Ephesus and then read in the congregation. Then it was probably read in all the congregations upriver from Ephesus, such as the congregation at Colossae.[13] Copies would have been made by Christians who had the ability and means to do so,

---

[10]Again, the Septuagint is often abbreviated as "LXX." Due to their dedication to the King James Only position, a few people deny that the New Testament writers used the LXX, but in the broad realm of New Testament scholarship this is not questioned.

[11]See, for example, the citation of Jeremiah 31:32 in Hebrews 8:9, taken not from the Hebrew Massoretic text but from the Greek Septuagint rendering of Jeremiah.

[12]John 10:35.

[13]Indeed, Paul is probably making reference to his letter to the Ephesians in Colossians 4:16.

and when visitors would come, visitors who had not previously encountered Paul's epistle, they would ask to make copies for their home churches. Some of these copies would travel far, far away from Ephesus. Some would even be lost in ancient collections, not to be seen again for millennia. But the point is that they would be distributed far and wide. Now, there are two results of how those original books were copied.

One is that many people believe the ancient church somehow "controlled" the text of Scripture, so that if an ancient leader or group wanted to "delete" a belief they no longer held, they could do so. *This is manifestly not the case.* Never was there a time when any man, group of men, or church "controlled" the scriptural text. Even if a group had decided to alter it, they could never gather up all the copies already in existence; the means of travel would preclude such an attempt even if one was launched, for distribution of the copies would far exceed anyone's ability to recover them all. So if such a major "editorial effort" were to take place, what would be the result? Let's say someone, five hundred years after Christ, gathered up a bunch of manuscripts and "erased" all references to a doctrine. When those manuscripts and those copied from them would later be compared to all the manuscripts this group could not revise, the alteration would stand out like a lighthouse in the darkness. Any addition or deletion would be *easily* detected. This is why the entire manuscript tradition is so important: Any "tampering," because of tenacity, is immediately apparent.

The other result of the means the Lord used to transmit the Scriptures to us over time is the presence of the very textual variations due to scribal error that I noted before. Since those who longed to own copies were not always professional copyists, they made errors, and, as I mentioned, we have the means of recognizing those errors in both individual manuscripts and families of manuscripts. The original readings are still present, even when there are a number of options for a given word or phrase, but the benefit of knowing that the text has not been edited in wholesale fashion, as some assert, far outweighs the work we must invest in the study of textual variants. When we remember that truth is not enunciated in only one passage where a variant occurs, we see God's wisdom in protecting His Word in this way.

CALEB: I've never heard of this. You're saying, then, that by comparing all these manuscripts, despite the variations introduced by the normal process of copying, any kind of major editing in any one manuscript or even a group of manuscripts would be easily seen? Have such studies been done?

JOSHUA: All the time, in fact. The past century has brought to light a whole spectrum of new evidence, ever more ancient manuscripts, and the discoveries have only *increased* our confidence in the text of the New Testament. You see, Caleb, if there *were* "plain and precious truths" removed from the Bible, we would have clear and compelling evidence thereof. The simple fact is you have to *assume* such degradation of the text and squish it all into the most unlikely limited time period to come up with the kind of corruption the *Book of Mormon* suggests.[14]

---

[14]Recent LDS scholarship has joined the attack upon the transmission of the biblical text. They point to a number of "facts" to substantiate the assault on the Bible, which is part of the text of the *Book of Mormon* (ironic, in light of the almost instantaneous corruption of *that* work's text even within the lifetime of its author). They cited various early "Christian" writings wherein the authors either quote from the canonical Scriptures in a *pesher* style (stringing quotes together that in most instances have little to do with each other in their original contexts) or cite from non-canonical works, some of which we possess, some we do not. These citations are assumed to demonstrate that the text of Scripture in the second century differed substantively from the form it had when the first manuscripts appeared in the historical record, a concept not unlike that offered by liberal higher criticism in centuries past (wherein they theorized a massive evolutionary change in the text of Scripture as Christian theology "evolved" into the fourth century, a theory refuted by the discovery of the earliest papyri, which give no evidence of such a process). They likewise refer to Peter's statement (2 Peter 3:15–16) that there are difficult things in Paul's letters that the untaught and unstable distort. Further, some early writers spoke of various groups (such as the Montanists or the Marcionites) trying to corrupt the Scriptures or making reference to the "secret gospel of Mark."

When faced with the actual manuscript evidence, these scholars seek to undermine its significance by pointing to well-known facts, such as that the bulk of these manuscripts are "late" (after the tenth century) and that only a few papyri can be dated to this early period. The very effort on the part of LDS scholars and apologists says much

AN ISLAMIC DIALOGUE

In May 1999 I had the privilege of debating Hamza Abdul Malik, a representative of the Islamic Propagation Center.[15] The debate took place in Syosset, New York, on Long Island. The topic was *slated* to be "Does the New Testament Teach the Deity of Christ?" but it became very clear that my opponent

about modern Mormonism, especially in light of its attempt to become mainstream. At any rate, the attempts fail reasoned analysis. (Indeed, if the same standards were applied to the LDS Scriptures, none of these writers would be able to hold to their authority or integrity. The wholesale editing of the LDS Scriptures is a documented fact. See Jerald and Sandra Tanner, *The Changing World of Mormonism* [Moody Press, 1980].)

In response to the assertions made above:

First, it is highly doubtful LDS scholars would accept the works of various modern-day writers who claim to stand in Joseph Smith's shoes, let alone consider their writings altogether relevant, and yet they (and most other such critics, no matter what their religious viewpoint) uncritically lump all *early* writings together as if they carry equal weight. We surely see that today untaught and unstable individuals do not refrain from putting their thoughts on paper, so why should it have been different in the early centuries? Indeed, the groups referenced by these writers, such as the Marcionites (gnostics who believed the God of the Old Testament was a demiurge, an evil god who was an emanation from the one true God), fit the descriptions given in the New Testament concerning false teachers. It is far more likely that these individuals were ignorant of what constituted the Scriptures than that they were accurately reflecting a completely different *form* of the scriptural text. (There is also another reason to reject this idea, which I will note below.)

Second, the very fact that Marcion was opposed by numerous writers demonstrates that his action of cutting up the text of Scripture was *not* the norm; his aberrant behavior was detected and rejected by sound believers.

Third, Peter's statement is not that the untaught and unstable distorted the *text* of Scripture, but that they distorted the *meaning* of Scripture to their own destruction.

Finally, the textual issues provide the most compelling argument against the position taken by LDS critics and others. Consider the result of the assertions being made: If there were, in fact, wholesale changes to the New Testament text, *where is the evidence of this when the New Testament text emerges in full form in the papyri and great early uncial texts?* (See my treatment of these issues in *The King James Only Controversy.*) Are we truly to believe that all of these tremendously altered texts, containing all these now lost "plain and precious truths," simply vanished or perhaps were taken by angels to heaven? No one copied them? Why not? If the manuscript tradition was as wildly divergent in the second century as is claimed, the beginning of the fourth century would present a hopelessly mangled mess of conflations and variations that would leave the text completely unintelligible. But is this what the documented evidence (rather than speculations based upon inferences from a wide range of sources) shows us? No. Even if the investigation is limited to the first five centuries of manuscripts, neither the Old nor New Testament gives *any* evidence of this kind of wholesale textual alteration, insertions and deletions, and the like. This is the greatest evidence against the theory presented; again, if the theory were true, the state of the text at the beginning of the fourth century, for example, would be *massively* different than it actually is.

[15]This debate, available in audio and video formats at *www.aomin.org,* is a valuable resource for helping Christians understand how a Muslim "hears" the evidence for the deity of Christ; the audience questions at the end of the evening provide extensive education in and of themselves.

had a different focus in mind. When faced with the mountain of scriptural evidence for the deity of Christ, his response was telling: Any and all passages in the Bible that teach the deity of Christ were *inserted later.* That is, the real reason Mr. Malik engaged in this debate was for the chance to tell Christians that the Bible has been corrupted over time. The following direct transcript of a section during cross-examination exemplifies exactly how many modern Muslims view the Bible in light of their preexisting beliefs.

WHITE: Sir, you closed your last statement by saying that both the end of Matthew and the testimony of John should not be relied upon because you allege that they are contradictory. Is this not an admission on your part [that] the New Testament *does* teach the deity of Christ, but you reject those sections that, in fact, testify to His deity?

MALIK: No, no. It's not that at all. I'm saying if something is contradictory, then the trust in it is lost right away. You can't trust it.

WHITE: Are the—

MALIK: In a court of law, it would not be admitted as evidence. These scriptures, in a modern-day court of law, if two witnesses came with those kind of stories, they would be discredited.

WHITE: Are the passages in Matthew 28:19–20 . . . is the passage in the New Testament?

MALIK: 28:19–20?

WHITE: Uh-huh.

MALIK: It's there, yes.

WHITE: And . . .

MALIK: And I'm saying, based on my study, that it's interpolated scripture.

WHITE: And . . . so you believe that it's been added in later.

MALIK: Yes.

WHITE: Do you have a single manuscript from any of the 5,300 copies of the Greek manuscripts of the New Testament that substantiates that assertion?

MALIK: Well, first of all, Mark ends his gospel with pretty much the same words. "Go ye into all the word and preach the gospel to every creature." However, Mark did not mention baptizing [in] the name of the Father, Son, and the Holy Ghost. Had Jesus told him that, had that . . . had he been inspired to make that statement, in no way, something so valid to the missionary work would he have overlooked that.

WHITE: So you—

MALIK: Had no one other than Mark wrote, you would have never known to baptize in the name of the Father, Son, and the Holy Spirit.

WHITE: So your assertion is that unless Matthew, Mark, Luke, and John read exactly the same, then they must be contradictory with one another?

MALIK: No, I'm saying that Jesus never taught that, and so the church, the early church had to get that doctrine in, so they added that doctrine in.

WHITE: So do you know of a single manuscript, sir, anywhere in the world, that does not contain Matthew 28:19–20?

MALIK: I know that they're there, but then I know, I know also, that that injunction was not carried out.

WHITE: So, sir, my question is very simple. Is there or is there not a single shred of factual historical information to substantiate what you're asserting, that this is an addition to the text?

MALIK: Certainly, I don't know of manuscripts, but I read scholars who are specialists in that field, and they have looked at those manuscripts and seen a lack of them there—

WHITE: Could you give me one name?

MALIK: . . . and they have written . . . no, I can't give you that now, but the point is . . . here's my point now. I'm saying to you that Matthew 28:19, because Jesus never taught any baptizing, He didn't teach anybody to do that. He never baptized Himself and never taught anyone to do that. He didn't teach anybody the doctrine of Trinity. . . .

WHITE: So based on your understanding . . .

MALIK: . . . and He didn't give a great commission. He never gave a great commission. Jesus says in Matthew 15:24, "I personally am sent only to the lost sheep of the house of

Israel." He never ever changed that statement concerning Himself—

WHITE: Except for the passage that you reject.

MALIK: No, no, not that. That's not for Himself. That's for His apostles. He never changed it for Himself, ever.

WHITE: Okay.

MALIK: Not one place. Now, in Matthew 10:5–6, it said that He gave a limited commission to His apostles, "Go ye into all . . . go not in the way of the Gentiles or any city of the Samaritans but go rather to the lost sheep of Israel."

WHITE: After His resurrection, yes.

MALIK: Now, because there was no great commission—

WHITE: Sir, we're getting off the question I'm asking. I'm trying to be very focused here, sir. I'm asking a very specific question. Is it your assertion that every place the term *God* is used of Jesus—and you have not addressed any of them yet—that every place the term *God* is used of Jesus—Romans 9:5; Titus 2:13; John 1:1—that each one of them is an interpolation and has, in fact, been added to the text of the New Testament?

MALIK: Yeah, they're fabrications.

WHITE: And can you show me—

MALIK: When someone is applying "God" to Jesus, "God" to Jesus as divinity, then I'm saying that does not—

WHITE: So your assumption determines what is Scripture rather than Scripture determining what your conclusions will be?

MALIK: No, I'm saying basic fundamental of scripture, the rule of interpretating [*sic*] scripture is that the rule is anything that is subject to various interpretations cannot be interpreted as to contradict something basically fundamental. Now, I'm saying what is basically fundamental from Genesis to Revelation is that God is one with no [unintelligible], no likeness or equal. That is fundamental.

WHITE: That's your assumption.

MALIK: But we have—

WHITE: That's your assumption. You—

MALIK: What I'm saying . . .

WHITE: You know, that came from the Qur'an, didn't it? It didn't come from the Bible, did it?

MALIK: No, no, no, that's . . . biblical scholars, any scholar that approaches Scripture, knows that when you talk about allegories . . . metaphors . . . that you don't give those understandings that contradict things that are very plain in that same thing.

WHITE: So is John 1:1 a part of the New Testament?

MALIK: I'm saying . . . John 1:1 is there, but it goes against the doctrine of the Synoptic Gospels.

WHITE: Does John 1:1 teach the deity of Christ?

MALIK: And it doesn't. John 1:1 does . . . in some sense . . .

WHITE: So if John 1:1 . . .

MALIK: . . . depends on . . . depends on the interpretation, because in the earlier scriptures, in the early 1500s, I think it was [William] Tyndale or somebody. . . .

WHITE: Tyndale . . .

MALIK: Tyndale . . . when he translated that Scripture, he said, "In the beginning was the Word, and the word was with God, and Word was God and it." He uses "it". . . .

WHITE: That's fine.

MALIK: "It." You know that?

WHITE: Yes I do.

MALIK: And now—

WHITE: It was common English usage at the time.

MALIK: The point now is that it's being used as "He." It's given a masculine gender when it . . .

WHITE: Well, it is a masculine gender.[16] But sir, so the point is, John 1:1 teaches the deity of Christ; John 1:1 is in the New Testament. Why should I not say that the thesis of the debate has now been established, and you have admitted the New Testament does teach the deity of Christ? You simply believe, given your presuppositions coming from another perspective, that we have to reject those Scriptures because it's not in accordance with your belief?

---

[16]The Greek term used is masculine.

MALIK: No, no, no. You see, up to this debate my first mind was to say to you, no, let's argue does Jesus Himself teach His divinity? But I allowed this to go because I wanted to establish before you and the audience that the New Testament teaches both ways, that it teaches the deity of Christ and it teaches that He's not. So now we have to figure out which one is sound. I'm saying that because this Scripture has been interpolated, that someone is teaching a doctrine that Jesus is deity against the basic flow of the Bible that teaches is not God. God is—

WHITE: Okay, can you show me a single manuscript that deletes John 1:1, Colossians 1:15, or any of the others?

MALIK: No, no, no, why are you asking me about manuscripts?

WHITE: Because I'm asking for historical evidence, sir. You're making an assertion based upon your understanding of Scripture. I don't believe you, or, I could claim to be infallible. Therefore, we could be wrong in our understanding. The question then is, what does the New Testament write . . . actually read? And that is an area of my expertise. And I do know what the New Testament reads. I have a critical edition right here. If you'd like to point me to any early manuscript of the New Testament that long predates the rise of Islam that does not contain these passages I'd like to see it.

MALIK: That's no problem, they're there, but I'm just saying—

WHITE: Where, sir?

MALIK: I'm saying that they're contradicted by other passages in the Bible as well. That's all I'm saying to you.

WHITE: Okay. Could you explain why the apostle Paul would describe Jesus Christ as the Creator of all things, in these words: "For by Him all things were created both in the heavens and on earth, visible and invisible, whether thrones or dominions or rulers or authorities, all thing were created through Him and for Him. He is before all things, and in Him all things hold together." Is that something you'd use to describe a creature?

MALIK: It certain[ly] isn't, and I wouldn't understand why he would say that, having said in Romans 1:3 that Jesus was born of the seed of David according to the flesh.

WHITE: If you understood, however, that we need to accept everything the New Testament teaches, and that Jesus Christ is the God-man, then those passages are not contradictory, are they?

MALIK: I don't understand . . . Jesus first of all, because of [the term] *anthropos,* is a God-man. I've said that . . . from His words. These are His words now. We're not talking about Paul or anyone else, or the gospel writers. We see out of the mouth of Jesus comes the negate any possibility of His being a God-man.

WHITE: How do you know that Jesus said *anthropos* in John 8:40 if you don't believe that the New Testament is actually accurate? [audience laughter]

MALIK: Well, I'll take your word. If you reject it, I'll reject it also, it's no problem.

At this point it was hard to know how to proceed, since it was painfully obvious that, as far as the debate was concerned, the issue had been resolved. No matter what passage I would address, it would be dismissed as "interpolated Scripture." The rest of the debate was mainly on Mr. Malik's allegations of contradiction in the biblical text.

CONCLUSION

While much more could be said about the history and transmission of the text of Scripture,[17] the key element to remember for the believer who faces ever-increasing hostility toward the Bible is this: God has preserved His Word over time in fulfill-

---

[17]Numerous resources exist to provide further insight into the process of the transmission of the text of Scripture. I address many elements of this issue in *The King James Only Controversy.* Likewise, Norman Geisler and William Nix in *A General Introduction to the Bible* (Moody Press, 1986) provide excellent background information. Other basic introductions include F. F. Bruce's *The Books and the Parchments* (Revell, 1984) and his popular *The New Testament Documents: Are They Reliable?* (Eerdmans, 1980); see also Bruce M. Metzger's *The New Testament: Its Background, Growth and Content* (Abingdon, 1983) and his more technical *The Text of the New Testament: Its Transmission, Corruption, and Restoration* (Oxford, 1980).

ment of His promise to His church. The very same divine power that moved holy men of old to speak from God, resulting in the God-breathed Scriptures, has been providentially active in preserving them from the ravages of the enemies of God's people. His purposes cannot be thwarted, and one of those purposes includes the presence of His Word in His church, among His people. Given that God's purposes never fail (Psalm 33:10–11), the one who asserts the corruption of the Word needs to explain why God would allow His Word to be snatched from His people against His will. Very few would even attempt to substantiate such a concept from the pages of the Bible.

Any person who seeks on one hand to claim some level of fidelity to Christ and the Scriptures, while on the other attacking the consistency, accuracy, and validity of the Bible, clearly has an external authority at work, one that does not find its basis in Christian teaching and must, as a result, denigrate the centrality of scriptural authority. Ironically, one can almost always detect these external authorities at work with only a small amount of effort. It has been my experience that those religious groups that attack the Bible's transmission over time will hold to some form of authority (either other Scriptures, such as the LDS Church's *Book of Mormon,* or in the form of tradition, such as Roman Catholicism's claims) that, when tested fairly and on the same basis as the Bible, cannot possibly pass the test. The double standard is a glowing red flag that all is not well.

CHAPTER 8

Allegations

of

Contradiction

The theological necessity of inerrancy as the counterpart to Scripture's very nature leads to a discussion of the many allegations of contradiction within the biblical text. Theological paradigms are fine, but if they result in factual claims incapable of surviving fair and honest examination, those paradigms are shown to be worthless. Inerrancy most *definitely* results in particular factual claims regarding the text of Scripture; specifically, if the Scriptures are an inspired, infallible, inerrant revelation of God's truth, then they will not be self-contradictory. This mark of truthfulness will extend not only to doctrinal issues but to factual issues as well; it will not do to suggest that God would choose to use factually or historically false words to convey eternal truths. Popular or not, such a view of Scripture is incoherent and indefensible.

And so we must be willing to engage the sometimes difficult, often challenging, and always rewarding task of responding to alleged contradictions in the text of Scripture. We do so not out of a desire to be argumentative but so that we may remove cavils against God's Word that are not founded upon truth. We do so to clarify God's claims and to remove obstructions to faith. We do so out of a Spirit-borne conviction that what we are reading is truly God's Word, and, as Jesus said, "Your word is truth" (John 17:17).

The single best defense of Scripture has already been given: sound exegesis of the text that allows it to speak in the context of its own authors.[1] *The vast majority of allegations of contradiction are the result of misinterpretation.* If the rules of hermeneutics were allowed to function consistently, most "Bible contradiction" publications and Web sites would quickly wither. But we can hardly be surprised that atheists or even others do not allow for the fair handling of the biblical text when most evangelicals only learn about hermeneutics in passing, through comments made from the pulpit (in opposition to direct teaching), and many mainline denominations not only allow liberal, anti-supernaturalist scholars to teach in their seminaries, but they also promote their conclusions and spread their views through the denominational publications. As already noted, believing in inerrancy is as popular as interpreting the Constitution as our founding fathers intended it; most "scholarship" has moved past such notions, and the results are dire.

Obviously, the first thing to keep in mind in any conversation over the subject of *contradiction* is the actual definition of the term. Having two sources say the same thing in different words is not a contradiction. Having one author choose to include a different set of facts in his recounting of an incident than another author is not a contradiction. Having one author give more information than another author is not a contradiction. Having one author discuss a situation in another context, and hence having a different emphasis in his relating it than another, is not a contradiction. A contradiction is easily defined: Stated briefly, the law of noncontradiction is that A and *non-A* cannot both be true at the same time and in the same sense. A contradiction involves asserting that A is true *and* that non-A is true, at the same time and in the same context. It

---

[1]See chapter 4.

is not saying that A is true and A can be seen in a different light in a different context. It is also not saying that A is true and non-A may be true by looking at the situation from another angle. This basic definition of *contradiction* is rarely allowed to hold its meaning when it comes to criticism of the Bible.

Contradiction can exist *inherently* in a text (i.e., the words actually express contradictory statements) or it can exist in an errant *reading* of a text (i.e., a person may read a text in such a way as to introduce contradiction through misunderstanding). Again, this is the primary source of alleged biblical contradictions; it may not require ill will and may simply come from any number of sources of personal or corporate ignorance. If ignorant of the meanings of words, instead of seeking a term's definition as it was used by the author, the critic may read into it an anachronistic and therefore errant interpretation. Defining words as they would be understood in a modern context is one of the most common errors of critics of the scriptural text.

Some critics of the Bible likewise base their comments upon English translations rather than the original documents, introducing further anachronistic misunderstandings and errors. It is one thing to prove a problem with a translation, for translations by nature are not inerrant; it is quite another to say this proves an error in the original. One might find an inconsistency in a Russian translation of the U.S. Constitution, but that error does not invalidate the English original, *unless the same contradiction exists in the original* and the Russian translation is simply communicating that error accurately. This is a particular trap for monolingual critics unfamiliar with the issues involved in translating from one language to another. Likewise, monolingual believers often find it difficult to handle such arguments, for they are unable to directly access information that would expose the supposed problem. Further, it is often said, "The gospel is for everyone, not just scholars," as if this somehow means we never need to deal with the original languages or else sacrifice the clarity or simplicity of the gospel. Regardless, answering critics is not the same as proclaiming the gospel message, and if objections to the faith go to the level of the original languages, then we need to deal with those issues.

Anachronism can exist when dealing with such factors as the historical setting and backgrounds of the Scriptures as well. This is especially true when people attempt to force the Bible into conformity with modern, scientific categories that came into existence and usage long after God's Word was recorded. Of course, Christians are guilty of attempting to eisegetically read into many passages scientific concepts that are just as anachronistic and misrepresentative of the text as the alleged errors of the atheists, so at some level we are guilty of bolstering our opponents, so to speak. As noted before, we should be consistent and always insist that God's Word be handled aright so that we honor Him, His authority, and His Word by hearing Him.

PRACTICAL INERRANCY ILLUSTRATED

One of the most effective ways of defending inerrancy is providing examples of how common allegations betray an unfair bias on the part of the person seeking to find biblical errors. Dialogue between Joshua and an atheist we'll call "Dennis" will serve as the vehicle of our demonstration. Dennis is a composite of many atheists with whom I have conversed over recent years, and his brusque character is an accurate reflection of the kind of dialogue one can expect when dealing with this particular issue.

DENNIS: Your Bible, aside from originating in a world of mythology and scientific ignorance, is likewise filled with internal self-contradictions that defy explanation.

JOSHUA: Oh? I've seen a number of *suggested* contradictions, but I have never seen one successfully *proven* in a fair manner.

DENNIS: Well, allow me to help you see the light. Let's start with an obvious one demonstrating the Bible's scientific illiteracy. The Old Testament says that the Israelites were to eat only "clean" animals. One of the rules Jehovah gave them concerned chewing the cud, and Leviticus 11:6 says the rabbit is forbidden, "for though it chews cud, it does not divide the hoof, it is unclean to you." Now, whoever penned these words failed Biology 101, because rabbits do not chew the cud. Their digestive system does not have the necessary equipment.

JOSHUA: That's actually true. But I thank you for providing a wondrous example of how *not* to read an ancient text in a fair or logical manner.

DENNIS: How was I unfair?

JOSHUA: You are defining "chew the cud" in the modern sense of being a *ruminant,* an animal with a digestive system that allows for further digestion of the food at a later time after eating, correct?

DENNIS: Of course. What else could it mean?

JOSHUA: Let's think about it for a second. God is giving His law to Israel so that they can fulfill their role as His chosen people. That law has to be in some fashion *usable* to those to whom it is given, correct? Now, demanding of the Israelites a modern taxonomic knowledge of ruminants and their digestive system is plainly anachronistic, isn't it? When you look at a rabbit from a distance, does it not appear to be undertaking the same kind of action as a ruminant, that is, chewing the cud? Does its mouth not move in the same fashion? And isn't that the only means an Israelite would have of knowing one way or the other?

DENNIS: But that's not chewing the cud!

JOSHUA: The Hebrew phrase does not communicate what your modern mind would like to force into it. In the context of the Israelite observing a rabbit, it would appear to him that the rabbit is clean because of the motion of its mouth when eating. But the law excludes it on another basis. Your assertion, as I said, is illustrative of refusing to allow the text to speak in its own context and on its own basis.

DENNIS: I hardly think so, but if you don't like that example, then let's go to your precious Paul. He couldn't seem to keep his stories straight. Let me read his own words to you from the venerable King James:

> And the men which journeyed with him stood speechless, hearing a voice, but seeing no man. [2]

---

[2]Acts 9:7.

And they that were with me saw indeed the light, and were afraid; but they heard not the voice of him that spake to me. [3]

In one place Paul says they heard a voice, in the other he says they did not. Which is it?

JOSHUA: And here I thought you might have something new, Dennis! This is one of the oldest ones out there. Let's work through this—it's an important passage.

DENNIS: I would love to hear an explanation of this one.

JOSHUA: This is an excellent example of a situation where the original words must be allowed to be heard in the argument; if we do not allow this, we could falsely charge Luke with a mistake he did not make. First, I note you used the King James Version. We need to observe that some modern versions translate the passage differently.

DENNIS: Oh, there's always a way around it from the "translation" angle.

JOSHUA: I surely do not want to "get around it," but I also happen to know that the original language differs between the two texts, [4] so the translation should reflect this. Note the NIV, for example:

The men traveling with Saul stood there speechless; they heard the sound but did not see anyone. [5]

My companions saw the light, but they did not understand the voice of him who was speaking to me. [6]

DENNIS: That's convenient.

JOSHUA: Actually, it's good translation. The proper question is, does the underlying text support the differentiation between "hearing" and "understanding" that the NIV reflects? Let me show you from the Greek text the important phrases:

9:7 is *akouontes men tes phones;*
22:9 is *ten de phonen ouk ekousan tou lalountos moi.*

---

[3]Acts 22:9.
[4]Acts 9:7 and 22:9.
[5]Acts 9:7.
[6]Acts 22:9.

First, in 9:7 *akouo,* the verb that means "to hear," is a nominative plural participle; in 22:9 it is a plural aorist verb.

Second, in 9:7 *phone,* a "sound" or "voice," is a singular genitive noun; in 22:9 it is a singular accusative noun.

Third, in 9:7 *akouo* precedes its object; in 22:9 it follows its object.

Fourth, in 9:7 the phrase is not modified; in 22:9 it is modified by "of the one speaking to me."

Finally, in 9:7 Luke is narrating an event in Greek; in 22:9 Paul is speaking to a crowd in Hebrew or Aramaic.

Dennis, you are in an impossible position here. You cannot force the argument, for the differences between the two passages are quite significant, so the argument must proceed on the grounds of contradictory meanings only; the grammar of the two passages will not support a clear "A vs. non-A" proposition.

DENNIS: I don't claim to read the original languages, but it strikes me as very odd that the two accounts would be so different. The King James translators evidently didn't see what you see.

JOSHUA: It's doubtful anyone had ever raised the issue, but be that as it may, the real question is, do we have a solid basis upon which to assert that Paul meant the men heard a sound but did not understand what the voice was saying? I believe we do, and I am not alone on this. Numerous Greek scholars have said the very same thing: [7] They all refer to the possibility that the case difference of *akouo* between 9:7 and 22:9 points to a difference in meaning. However, as Dr. A. T. Robertson noted, this distinction cannot be written in stone, so why do I believe I am correct in asserting this difference as the answer to your supposed contradiction? One word: *context.* I don't know how deeply you have studied this text, but I have spent a fair amount of time on it, due to its frequent presentation by those who deny biblical inerrancy.

---

[7]For instance, see W. E. Vine, *Expository Dictionary of New Testament Words* (Bethany House, 1984); A. T. Robertson, *Word Pictures in the New Testament,* (Baker, 1930), 3:117–18; James Hope Moulton, *A Grammar of New Testament Greek* (T & T Clark, 1985), I:66; Nigel Turner, *Grammatical Insights Into the New Testament* (T & T Clark, 1966), III:233.

The key element with which you'll need to come to grips is noted by scholars who have pored over these passages.[8] In Acts 22:9, Paul is speaking to a crowd in Jerusalem; according to Acts 21:40, Paul addressed the crowd in Hebrew.

DENNIS: The NIV here says Aramaic.[9]

JOSHUA: Closely related, and the difference would not impact this point. Paul mentions to his Hebrew listeners that when Jesus called him, he called him in Hebrew. How do we know this? In both Acts 9:4 and in Acts 22:7 "Saul" is not spelled in its normal form but is spelled in its Hebrew or Aramaic form—"Saoul." This tells us that the "voice" spoke in Hebrew; therefore, Acts 22:9 teaches that the men who accompanied Paul did not understand what was said because they could not understand Hebrew. The text strongly supports this, for again, Paul modifies "they did not hear[10] the voice" by adding, "of the one speaking to me." The emphasis is on the speaking of the voice, which indicates comprehension and understanding. Now, given the above scholars' citations and the context of the passages, can anyone seriously deny that there is a perfectly plausible explanation for this supposed contradiction?

DENNIS: Hey, if you have to dive deep into the original languages and the rest, I guess that says something in and of itself, doesn't it?

JOSHUA: Actually, if you grasped this issue, Dennis, many of your favorite alleged contradictions would evaporate into thin air. Part and parcel of dealing with almost any ancient or even modern writing is the basic idea that the author gets the benefit of the doubt. It is highly unlikely that a writer will contradict himself within short spans of time or space. Luke was a careful historian, and it is sheer speculation that he would be so forgetful as to not remember what he wrote in Acts 9 by the time he wrote Acts 22. The person who will

---

[8]Specifically, see R. J. Knowling, *Expositor's Greek Testament* (Eerdmans, 1983) 2:231–33; and John Aberly, *New Testament Commentary* (Board of Publication of the United Lutheran Churches of America, 1936), 414.
[9]"Here" meaning Acts 22:2; cf. 26:14.
[10]"Understand."

not allow for textual harmonization is in effect claiming omniscience of all the facts surrounding an event that took place nearly two millennia ago; most careful scholars do not make such claims. The explanation I have given you is perfectly reasonable, it coincides with the known facts, and it does not engage in unwarranted special pleading.[11] If you wish to persist in claiming that Acts 9:7 contradicts Acts 22:9, Dennis, there is little I can do about it. But realize that, first, your position cannot be proven; second, you are operating on unproven assumptions, such as that Luke was not intelligent enough to notice a contradiction in his own writing; and third, there is a perfectly logical explanation based on the original languages and contexts.

DENNIS: I suppose that's how you'd also reply to why the Bible can't seem to get it straight about whether the command is not to *murder* or not to *kill?*

JOSHUA: Let me guess, another issue about King James rendering?

DENNIS: Hey, it's used by most of the fundamentalists I talk to, so why not? Compare Matthew 19:18 with Romans 13:9:

> Jesus said, Thou shalt do no murder, Thou shalt not commit adultery, Thou shalt not steal, Thou shalt not bear false witness.
> Thou shalt not commit adultery, Thou shalt not kill, Thou shalt not steal, Thou shalt not bear false witness, Thou shalt not covet.

So which is it? Killing isn't necessarily murder, but the Bible says we're not to do either one, which makes no sense.

JOSHUA: What makes no sense, Dennis, is how many folks like yourself do not apply the same standards to the Bible that you would expect to be applied to your own writings or to any other historical document. The very first question in your mind should be, "What did Matthew write, and what

---

[11] *Special pleading* is a logical fallacy wherein a double standard is employed by the person making the assertion. Special pleading typically happens when one insists upon less strict treatment for the argument one is making than one would make when evaluating another's argument.

did Paul write?" especially since both of them are citing the same commandment. The answer is not difficult to discover, even for someone who hasn't studied the original languages. Both passages are quoting the Greek Septuagint, and the commandment is identical in both passages.

DENNIS: Then why does the King James translate it differently?

JOSHUA: It's a simple matter of history. The King James Version was translated by committees that met at various places between 1604 and 1611. The Gospels were translated by a different group than the Pauline epistles; when their work was done, it was reviewed but imprecisely edited. Modern translations render the two passages identically because the Greek texts are identical; the differing translations should have been harmonized in the KJV, but they were not. So your argument carries no more weight than to prove that English-translation editors are not infallible, which, of course, has nothing to do with the Bible itself. Truly, Dennis, if something you wrote was translated into another language decades or even centuries from now, would you find it fair to be accused of having been inconsistent and self-contradictory just because an editor of that translation did not perfectly smooth everything out before it was published?

DENNIS: I doubt anything I've written will ever be translated into another language, so I won't worry about it. Okay, how about all the contradictions among Matthew, Mark, and Luke?

JOSHUA: I assume you are referring to the so-called "Synoptic Problem," the issues that arise from comparing the Gospel accounts of the various events in Christ's ministry?

DENNIS: Yeah, loads of contradictions there.

JOSHUA: Many believe so, yes, but again I remind you that *contradiction* is a term with a specific meaning and definition that requires more on your part than mere allegation.

DENNIS: Fine. Here's an obvious one: Mark 6:8 and Luke 9:3:

He instructed them that they should take nothing for their

journey, except a mere staff—no bread, no bag, no money in
their belt.

He said to them, "Take nothing for your journey, neither a
staff, nor a bag, nor bread, nor money; and do not even have
two tunics apiece."

This time you can't pull any Matrix-like "I'm Neo and I
know Greek" moves on me. This is a classic "X vs. non-X"
contradiction.

JOSHUA: It appears so, doesn't it? That's why I'm glad we've
been provided with a third source of the same saying.
Indeed, we might learn from this example not to judge
those instances in which we only have two accounts and find
them in apparent conflict. See, the third recording of Jesus'
instructions helps us to understand the two you just cited.
This is found in Matthew 10:9–10:

Do not acquire gold, or silver, or copper for your money
belts, or a bag for your journey, or even two coats, or sandals,
or a staff; for the worker is worthy of his support.

Matthew gives an expanded account, and in so doing he
provides the needed explanation as well. Jesus is instructing
the disciples to go out into ministry with the barest of neces-
sities, not looking to *acquire* anything extra for the trip.
When He tells them not to take shoes, do we really think
He means that they're to go barefoot? Of course not.
Rather, they are not to take *an extra pair* of shoes along. In
the same way, if a disciple had a staff, he would not be pro-
hibited from taking it along; if he did not have one, he was
not to *acquire* one just for the journey. So what we have in
Luke and Mark is only part of what we have in Matthew:
Luke records the prohibition given against acquiring
another staff, while Mark communicates the implicit permis-
sion to take along a staff *already* in possession. There is no
actual contradiction here.

DENNIS: Again, I find this sleight-of-hand very convenient. If
you didn't have Matthew, you'd never have a way out of that
one.

JOSHUA: It's not a matter of looking for a way out of something.

It's a matter of honestly dealing with the texts and allowing for harmonization between the accounts, something you'd allow for and expect in any modern situation where multiple witnesses to an event are recording their views. As this example shows, Mark and Luke were giving *complementary* not *contradictory* information, and the allegation of error actually lies in our ignorance of the statements' contexts. Matthew clears up the background in this instance, but what of those other instances where we don't have a third view? In honesty and fairness, should we not learn wisdom from this example and be slow to come to conclusions of contradiction?

DENNIS: Okay, so you can come up with a defense for what seems like the indefensible. But even Christian scholars admit the Bible has inconsistent teaching on basic issues. I am hardly isolated in concluding that Paul came up with his own religion and forced it on the early Christian movement, fundamentally hijacking its character and content. This isn't some cynical invention; it comes out in the obvious conflict between the teaching of James, which most closely parallels Jesus' teaching, and the teaching of Paul. They *are* in opposition, and some even think James is referring to Paul and *refuting* him in his comments.

JOSHUA: I see you've been doing some reading in postmodern humanist liberal theology—what a combination! You are quite correct in observing that there are those who believe Paul and James to be at odds. However, I see reason to believe that *neither* is Paul's teaching contradictory to or different from Jesus' teaching *nor* is James in conflict with Paul. Careful exegetes have concluded otherwise.

DENNIS: How could they? It's too obvious. James 2:20 and 24 says,

> Are you willing to recognize, you foolish fellow, that faith without works is useless? . . . You see that a man is justified by works and not by faith alone.

It seems James had Paul in mind, or at least those preaching Paul's message, as Romans 3:28 and 4:4–5 make clear:

We maintain that a man is justified by faith apart from works of the Law.

Now to the one who works, his wage is not credited as a favor, but as what is due. But to the one who does not work, but believes in Him who justifies the ungodly, his faith is credited as righteousness.

I'm sure you'll have an explanation, but every time I've heard a fundamentalist attempt a response to these passages I've gotten dizzy from all the loops and spins.

JOSHUA: Well, I can't convince you if you're beyond reason, Dennis. But I have, in fact, spent a great deal of time on this issue,[12] since it touches on the gospel itself. But here again you need to allow the original authors the freedom to say what they say *within their own context* and not that of your choosing. Do you think that the contexts of Romans 3–4 and James 2 are identical?

DENNIS: The word *to justify* is the same, I know that much.

JOSHUA: Yes, and the word *God* is the same between "God created the heavens and the earth" and "There is no God,"[13] but obviously words are defined on the basis of their usage and context. Are you convinced that Paul, speaking of how a man is justified before God, is addressing the same issue as James? That both men are addressing the same groups, the same concerns?

DENNIS: You clearly don't think so.

JOSHUA: Of course not, because I've taken the time to look at the texts. The subject in Romans is the grand work of God in Christ whereby He makes men right with Himself, establishing peace through *justification* by faith.[14] James is writing to Christians about how they are to live their lives *as believers.* One involves a focus upon what God has done in Christ, the other upon what our response should be in light of that work. One is written to Christians about the gospel, the other is written to Christians about how they are to live hav-

---

[12]Specifically, "James Attacks Empty Faith" in *The God Who Justifies* (Bethany House, 2001), 329–54.
[13]Genesis 1:1; Psalm 14:1.
[14]See Romans 5:1.

ing embraced that gospel. Beyond the completely different context, James tells us he is talking about a certain kind of empty faith, one that has no means of demonstrating its existence. You will note this section begins,

> What use is it, my brethren, if someone says he has faith but he has no works? Can that faith save him?[15]

Can *that* faith—a faith without external evidence of its existence—save? James say no, and Paul's answer is no as well. Note Paul's words to the Ephesians:

> We are His workmanship, created in Christ Jesus for good works, which God prepared beforehand so that we would walk in them.[16]

Both taught the same thing about the role of good works in the Christian life. Paul was not talking about that subject in the passages you cited from Romans; he was referring to one's entrance into a right relationship with God. God's grace cannot be joined to human works of merit. But James was not saying they could be either. He taught that living faith is able to demonstrate it exists outside the realm of mere words. Notice the concept of "showing," or "demonstrating":

> But someone may well say, "You have faith and I have works; show me your faith without the works, and I will show you my faith by my works."[17]

James's "show me" is in direct line with Paul's "God created you to live in a lifestyle that is marked by good works." Real faith can prove its existence, for faith that has no proof it exists through works is like a dead body that has no breath: breathing and life go hand in hand.

DENNIS: All right then, I should know better than to use an example that involves theology, because anyone can make the Bible say anything they want.

---

[15]James 2:14.
[16]Ephesians 2:10.
[17]James 2:18.

JOSHUA: Where have I misrepresented anything the text says, Dennis? I completely reject your assertion that anyone can make the Bible say what they want it to say. There is no question that many people twist Scripture to their own ends, but that is *misuse* of the Bible. Could I not take your own writings and misrepresent you by ignoring your context and intended meaning? That *I* can misuse your words does not mean *you* are inconsistent!

———

Unless the Spirit of God moves in the heart of an individual like Dennis, all the arguments in the world will not change his mind. We can seek to be sharp, useful instruments in the Master's hand and in the process grow in our love and knowledge of the Scriptures, but unless God removes the heart of stone and gives a heart of flesh (Ezekiel 36:26), no amount of argument will do. However, keep this in mind as well: When you give an answer for the hope that is in you (1 Peter 3:15), God is glorified, *even if you do not see the results!*

CHAPTER 9

Tradition, the Church, and the Development of Doctrine

For some reason, in God's providence, I recall with great clarity the first time anyone ever asked me about 2 Thessalonians 2:15 in the context of Roman Catholic claims regarding tradition. I was sitting at an "outreach dinner" at a very large Southern Baptist church, where I was an active member, when someone approached and asked how I would respond if shown the following text: "So then, brethren, stand firm and hold to the traditions which you were taught, whether by word of mouth or by letter from us." I do not recall the specifics of my response, but I do remember thinking it would be good to look more closely at the concept of "tradition" in its New Testament appearances.

In the years since I began actively responding to Rome's apologists and their denials of *sola scriptura*, I have heard 2 Thessalonians 2:15 cited hundreds of times as *prima facie* evidence of an extra-scriptural, non-written, oral form of tradition. Indeed, one of my most frequent opponents in debate, former Protestant minister Gerry Matatics, has repeatedly emphasized

that this passage is a command[1] and that only Roman Catholics
are obeying it since they are holding to *both* the written
traditions (the Scriptures) *and* the oral traditions. He claims
that Protestants by nature cannot do so, since we reject the
authority of oral tradition.[2] On this basis, he turns on its head
the normal charge made against Rome and accuses Protestants
of following a "manmade, unscriptural tradition." Since few
Protestants have spent much time on the passage in this context and have rarely heard a well-spoken defense of the Catholic position, it catches many off guard. The following dialogue
will illustrate this, hopefully stimulating insights that will be
helpful in providing a response.

ROBERT: It is all well and good, Joshua, to believe the Bible
alone is sufficient because of your particular understanding
of 2 Timothy 3:16,[3] but you need to approach the Bible as
a whole. The same apostle who wrote 2 Timothy 3:16 had
earlier commanded the Thessalonians to hold fast to two
forms[4] of tradition, oral and written. Read for me 2 Thessalonians 2:15, would you?

JOSHUA: Sure. "So then, brethren, stand firm and hold to the
traditions which you were taught, whether by word of
mouth or by letter from us."

ROBERT: If you check out the text, you will discover that the
word translated "hold to" is an imperative—a command. I
honestly believe, Joshua, that as a Catholic, I can hold to
this commandment, while you, as a Protestant, cannot. I
hold to both the oral tradition—that is, what Paul communicated by word of mouth, the teachings he delivered to the
Thessalonians—and the written form; that is, the Scriptures.

---

[1] It *is* a command, as both verbs, "stand fast" and "hold firmly to," are in the imperative mode.
[2] In reality, we *subject* oral tradition to the ultimate authority of Scripture in obedience to Jesus' example and command in Mark 7:5–13. See 1997 debate with Matatics on *sola scriptura* at *www.aomin.org*.
[3] "All Scripture is inspired by God and profitable for teaching, for reproof, for correction, for training in righteousness."
[4] Because the Second Vatican Council (Vatican II) did not use the formula "two sources of revelation" in regard to the written and oral forms of "tradition," many modern Catholics emphasize that there is *one source* with *two forms*. However, the phrase "two sources" has been used in Roman Catholic writings for centuries.

We Catholics hold to both, but you Protestants hold only to one.

JOSHUA: I'm familiar with the argument, though I confess you have confused me a bit. You've already said you believe in what you call "material sufficiency"; that is, all of God's revealed truths are at least implicitly contained in Scripture, rather than the *partim-partim* view, where God's truth is contained partly in the written tradition and partly in the oral traditions. Correct?

ROBERT: Yes, that is the most common Catholic view today. What's confusing about it?

Joshua: Well, Robert, I can see why a person who believes that some of what we need to know is found in Scripture and some in oral tradition would try to make use of 2 Thessalonians 2:15, but I don't see how your position is aided by it. You seem to believe that what Paul wrote in Scripture would have at least implicitly included what he taught them by preaching, right? So I don't understand why you would even bother with the reference.

ROBERT: Yes, it does indicate that there are two modes of revelation, an oral and a written.

JOSHUA: Obviously, during the time when the New Testament was still being enscripturated through the ministry of the apostles in the church, there is no doubt that the Word of God existed in both forms. That has never been the issue. The issue is, does this or any other passage lead us to believe that *after* the time of revelation, when the apostles had completed their mission and the Scriptures had come into existence and been entrusted to the church through the miraculous work of the Holy Spirit, there is to remain an orally passed down, unwritten component of the divine revelation? The words of 2 Thessalonians 2:15 do not even begin to indicate such an idea.

ROBERT: Why do you say that?

JOSHUA: This is really not an unusual or difficult passage. Paul had already commended the Corinthians in almost identical language in 1 Corinthians 11:2, which reads, "Now I praise you because you remember me in everything and *hold firmly to the traditions,* just as I delivered them to you."

ROBERT: And are you aware that the verb used there about passing these traditions down is a technical term related to tradition as well?

JOSHUA: Quite true, the verb is directly related to the noun. You could even say Paul "traditioned the traditions" to the Corinthians, Thessalonians, and so on. As a faithful steward, he passed on the truths he himself received, either directly from the Lord, as he often noted,[5] or as he had learned them from the apostles who had walked with Jesus. But in none of these passages are we given even a hint that the content of what is "traditioned" differs in the slightest from what Paul is writing to the churches. In fact, just the opposite is the case. What Paul spoke "in the presence of many witnesses" is what is to be passed on by the generations after he has gone.[6] This is not secret knowledge but is the very mark of Paul's public teaching. And what did Paul teach in the public places? Quite simply, the gospel.[7] Surely he went beyond the mere outline of the gospel in his preaching, but the gospel was the essence of his public proclamation.

ROBERT: Where do you get that from the text?

JOSHUA: Well, context is always preeminent. First, there is Paul's direct statement at the beginning of this very chapter,[8] leading us to believe that the oral and written components of Paul's message are not separate entities to be passed on in different ways. Note his words in verse 5: "Do you not remember that while I was still with you, I was telling you these things?" This already indicates the direct connection between the oral and the written. But there is more—let's back up to where Paul has spoken of the judgment of those who refuse to love the truth and then has contrasted them with the Thessalonians:

> But we should always give thanks to God for you, brethren beloved by the Lord, because God has chosen you from the beginning for salvation through sanctification by the Spirit and faith in the truth. And it was for this He called you through

---

[5]For example, Galatians 1:12; 1 Corinthians 11:23.
[6]2 Timothy 2:2.
[7]1 Corinthians 15:1–4 is a summarized statement.
[8]2 Thessalonians 2.

our gospel, that you may gain the glory of our Lord Jesus Christ.[9]

Unlike those who do not love the truth and are destroyed, God had chosen the Thessalonian believers *from the beginning* for salvation[10] by the Spirit and faith in the truth. This is the contrast that must be kept in mind between those who are perishing and those who are being saved in the previous verses. The Thessalonians know God has a purpose in calling them into the faith: "that you may gain the glory of our Lord Jesus Christ."

So Robert, the immediately preceding discourse is speaking of the gospel, of God's calling, and of the contrast between believers and unbelievers.

ROBERT: Again, all well and good, Joshua, but this *is* a command to hold to something, is it not?

JOSHUA: Yes, but it's a command that likewise leads us to believe Paul is simply exhorting us to continue steadfast in the truths already delivered by the apostles to the Thessalonians, and nothing more. As we discussed, there are two imperative verbs, "stand firm" and "hold fast." The first command is left without any elaboration, but since it is a common Pauline term, we're not left wondering what he means by it. He knew the Thessalonians would be able to understand this command from his regular usage of the term when he was among them. Note other places where he gives the same kind of command:

---

[9] 2 Thessalonians 2:13–14.

[10] A textual variant exists here, with a number of manuscripts reading "God chose you as the first fruits to be saved" rather than "from the beginning for salvation." The difference is small in the Greek (*aparchen* for "first fruits" versus *aparches* for "from the beginning"); because there were no spaces between words in the originals, the discrepancy is all of a single letter (in the Greek uncial script of the earliest manuscripts, APARXHN vs. APARXHS). In reality, there is little separation in meaning since both have "unto salvation," and the variant impacts the reading only by either telling us when God's decision took place (something already revealed elsewhere in Scripture; i.e., Ephesians 1:3–7) or telling us something about those who are chosen. "First fruits" is a popular word with Paul (e.g., Romans 8:23; 16:5; 1 Corinthians 15:20; 16:15), and for this reason many modern scholars prefer that reading. However, the external evidence only slightly favors "first fruits," so both readings should be considered.

Be on the alert, stand firm in the faith, act like men, be strong.[11]

For freedom Christ has set us free; stand firm therefore, and do not submit again to a yoke of slavery.[12]

Only conduct yourselves in a manner worthy of the gospel of Christ, so that whether I come and see you or remain absent, I will hear of you that you are standing firm in one spirit, with one mind striving together for the faith of the gospel.[13]

Therefore, my beloved brethren whom I long to see, my joy and crown, in this way stand firm in the Lord, my beloved.[14]

For now we really live, if you stand firm in the Lord.[15]

Note the phrases, Robert: Stand firm in the faith; stand firm against those who would mislead you; stand firm in one spirit, with one mind striving for the faith of the gospel; stand firm in the Lord. All of these phrases speak of Paul's exhortation to the Christian at war, the Christian battling the world, the flesh, and the devil. It speaks of one who refuses to give way, refuses to run when warring with the enemy. It is the constant refrain of the commander to his men in the face of the onslaught. And the foundation upon which the Thessalonians—and by extension, all believers—are to stand is very clear: stand firm in the faith, in the gospel, in the Lord.

ROBERT: Even so, you must admit *you* do not use the term *tradition* as Paul uses it here!

JOSHUA: It's true that in regular usage Protestants do not refer to tradition as often as we might, though I would say that's because of the term's misuse by your own communion, Robert. But this has no bearing on Paul's commanding the Thessalonians to hold firmly to the *traditions they had been taught.* Teaching was central to the apostle's ministry among

---

[11]1 Corinthians 16:13.
[12]Galatians 5:1 ESV.
[13]Philippians 1:27.
[14]Philippians 4:1.
[15]1 Thessalonians 3:8.

the churches; it was to be central to the continuation of the truth in the church as well.[16]

But here we come to the real issue: Can we know what Paul taught the Thessalonians? We can gain great insight by considering what he says in his first letter to them. He says they "received the word in much tribulation with the joy of the Holy Spirit."[17] He says he and the brethren had "the boldness in our God to speak to you the gospel of God amid much opposition,"[18] and likewise that they were more than happy to impart to the Thessalonians "not only the gospel of God but also our own lives."[19] He says that during his brief stay there he was exhorting and encouraging them, as a father does his own children, to "walk in a manner worthy" of the calling of God.[20] The message delivered to them was the very word of God, which is alive and active and working in believers.[21] Included in that ministry was instruction on how to walk and please God[22] and commandments regarding the necessity of godly behavior, and, in particular, sexual purity.[23] It is evident the apostle had at least briefly touched upon the coming of the Lord, but he felt some aspects of that topic needed further clarification.[24]

So may I insist, Robert, that the burden of proof lies squarely on the shoulders of the one who maintains that Paul communicated to the Thessalonians beliefs and doctrines *nowhere found in Scripture.* Do you believe Paul taught them such doctrines as papal infallibility or the immaculate conception of Mary?

ROBERT: Yes, Joshua, I believe he certainly taught them the basic truths that have now been defined by the Roman Catholic Church.[25]

---

[16]2 Timothy 2:2.
[17]1:6.
[18]2:2.
[19]2:8.
[20]2:11–12.
[21]2:13.
[22]4:1.
[23]4:2–4.
[24]4:13ff.
[25]Various answers may be given to this question. Those who follow the more modern

JOSHUA: And yet it is clear to Protestant and Catholic historians alike that there is no basis for believing that the Thessalonians, or anyone else in the days of Paul, believed such things. There is plenty of evidence that they believed in the gospel, in living worthy of their calling, and so forth, but none that they—or any Christians for literally centuries—believed anything remotely similar to the dogmas you seek to place within the use of the term *tradition* here in 2 Thessalonians.

CONCLUDING REMARKS

When dealing with this passage, no matter who is using it,[26] we must first understand it fully ourselves so as to communicate to others its central message. Paul is exhorting the Thessalonians to stand firm, unmoved, faithful to the teaching they had received from him in two forms: the spoken word when he was with them, and in his first epistle. These *traditions* encompass the gospel itself and the necessary results of confession of Christ as Savior (the "commandments" Paul speaks of in 1 Thessalonians regarding purity of behavior, walking worthily of the calling they had received from God). There is simply no substance in this passage for a secondary, extra-scriptural set of traditions to be passed down outside of Scripture. David King states,

> In 2 Thessalonians 2:15, Paul is simply binding the consciences of the Thessalonians to the content of his instruction regardless of the mode by which it was delivered. There

theories of John Henry Cardinal Newman, who promoted a theory of "development," would not believe that these entire dogmas were taught in the days of Paul. They liken the development of such truths to the acorn and the fully grown tree. The "acorn level of truth" would be referred to here that would eventually develop into the fully grown doctrines. But this is the voice of modern Rome; those Catholics who opposed the Reformation—though, ironically, not dogmatically believing papal infallibility or Mary's immaculate conception, both of which were defined as dogma centuries after Trent—believed the dogmas they defended had, in fact, been delivered by the apostles in a fashion almost identical to that of the Jews of Jesus' day, who believed their traditions had been passed down from Moses himself.

[26]Though I have not experienced this to be overly common, modern LDS apologists, seeking to find in early Christian history a basis for their own "unique" theology, may likewise make reference to such passages in seeking (like the Roman Catholic apologist) to undercut the truth of *sola scriptura*.

is no reason to believe that this text warrants any essential difference between the content of what Paul taught orally or by epistle.[27]

The phrase "by word of mouth" takes us back to that unique time in history when apostles walked the earth and God used them to build the foundation upon which the church has been built ever since.

SOLA SCRIPTURA VS. SOLO SCRIPTURA

In his book *The Shape of Sola Scriptura*,[28] Keith Mathison contrasts *sola scriptura* with what he calls *solo scriptura*. (Many of the criticisms he aims at *solo scriptura* have been enumerated above.) It is quite true that there are non-Catholics who wave the banner of *sola scriptura* as a veil to conceal their dislike of the Bible's teaching about the church, authority, and Christian truth. This is why holding to *sola scriptura* means one must likewise firmly hold to *tota scriptura*, belief in and acceptance of all that the Bible reveals. *Sola scriptura* is mocked when the entirety of the God-breathed revelation is not obediently read and followed, and, since the Scriptures speak of the church, teaching in the church, exhortation, rebuke, and the like, those who seek to make *sola scriptura* an excuse for being anti-church or simply heretical have no basis in the doctrine for their position. So I can join in this portion of the criticism of *solo scriptura*.

But on the other hand, does *sola scriptura* require us to believe that there is a "tradition" (or "rule of faith") to which we must appeal so as to have the correct interpretation of the Bible? There is no question that early Christian writers used this term, and many are quick to leap upon it with glee. But when we examine the term's meaning, we discover that most of the references were either to a basic, foundational outline of Christian belief concerning God and Christ, or to beliefs about practices and rites that were not doctrinal or dogmatic in nature. Irenaeus defined "tradition" as follows:

---

[27]David King and William Webster, *Holy Scripture: The Ground and Pillar of Our Faith*, (Christian Resources, 2001), 1:58.
[28]Keith Mathison, *The Shape of Sola Scriptura*, (Canon Press, 2001).

These have all declared to us that there is one God, Creator of heaven and earth, announced by the law and the prophets; and one Christ, the Son of God. If any one do not agree to these truths, he despises the companions of the Lord; nay more, he despises Christ Himself the Lord; yea, he despises the Father also, and stands self-condemned, resisting and opposing his own salvation, as is the case with all heretics.[29]

Obviously, the content of this "tradition" is not extra-scriptural: the Bible plainly teaches these things. Tertullian, writing later, gave an expanded version:

Now, with regard to this rule of faith—that we may from this point acknowledge what it is which we defend—it is, you must know, that which prescribes the belief that there is one only God, and that He is none other than the Creator of the world, who produced all things out of nothing through His own Word, first of all sent forth; that this Word is called His Son, and, under the name of God, was seen "in diverse manners" by the patriarchs, heard at all times in the prophets, at last brought down by the Spirit and Power of the Father into the Virgin Mary, was made flesh in her womb, and, being born of her, went forth as Jesus Christ; thenceforth He preached the new law and the new promise of the kingdom of heaven, worked miracles; having been crucified, He rose again the third day; [then] having ascended into the heavens, He sat at the right hand of the Father; sent instead of Himself the Power of the Holy Ghost to lead such as believe; will come with glory to take the saints to the enjoyment of everlasting life and of the heavenly promises, and to condemn the wicked to everlasting fire, after the resurrection of both these classes shall have happened, together with the restoration of their flesh. This rule, as it will be proved, was taught by Christ, and raises amongst ourselves no other questions than those which heresies introduce, and which make men heretics.[30]

---

[29]In Alexander Roberts and James Donaldson, eds., *The Ante-Nicene Fathers*, 1:414–415.
[30]Tertullian, *The Prescription Against Heretics*, 13.

But again, this can all be derived from the inspired text and does not exist as a separate revelation outside of Scripture. If all one means when speaking of the "apostolic tradition" and "interpreting the Scriptures in light of the rule of faith" is that certain nonnegotiables are foundational to a proper understanding of God's Word and the Christian faith, there can hardly be any argument. All one need do to see this truth is note the relatively few attempts made by LDS scholars to provide exegetical commentary on the text of Scripture, especially of the New Testament literature, and the impossibility of such a task in light of a belief in polytheism. One must understand the most basic outlines of Christian truth to delve more deeply into the revelation of Scripture, and if one begins with errors at that point, the rest of one's efforts will be in vain. If this is all that is meant by "the rule of faith," then such is completely understandable.

In fact, we could go one step further and say that the rule of faith represents the summary of apostolic doctrine that existed even during the time when the New Testament documents were being written. This rule of faith coincides with the text for the obvious reason that the apostles were the authors of both, though it should be noted that their written testimony in Scripture is more sure (and more specific) than the rule of faith. It is eminently logical to assume that as the New Testament was being written a summary of Christian truth *was* known and circulated; however, it is here that we again see the wisdom of God in the means He used to give Scripture. In contrast to the dependability and verifiability of the written biblical manuscripts, passing on of tradition by word of mouth is inherently subject to corruption and that very quickly.

A particularly striking example of this is provided in what may well be the first documented instance of a Christian writer specifically claiming to have information derived not from Scripture but orally from the apostles via "tradition." When Irenaeus sought to refute the arguments of the second-century gnostics, he made reference to a particular element of one of their arguments, and frankly, he missed the boat. Their argument was irrelevant, and his response was errant; in attempting to refute them, Irenaeus posited that Jesus was more than fifty years old when He died upon Calvary; he also asserted that since Christ came to save infants and children, boys and youths, and old men, He also had to go through all those stages of life Himself. How can Irenaeus prove Jesus was this old? By insisting that he was informed by those who knew the apostles:

> Now, that the first stage of early life embraces thirty years, and that this extends onwards to the fortieth year, every one will admit; but from the fortieth and fiftieth year a man begins to decline towards old age, which our Lord possessed while He still fulfilled the office of a Teacher, even as the Gospel and all the elders testify; those who were conversant in Asia with John, the disciple of the Lord, [affirming] that John conveyed to them that information. And he remained among them up to the times of Trajan. Some of them, moreover, saw not only John, but the other apostles also, and heard the very same account from them, and bear testimony as to the [validity of] the statement. Whom then should we rather believe?[31]

Note what Irenaeus claims, for church history is filled with this kind of error. There is no textual reason to believe Jesus was more than fifty years of age, yet Irenaeus claims "the Gospel" as *part* of his view's foundation. He quickly adds weight by saying "and all the elders." He buttresses his claim by insisting that "those who were conversant in Asia with John, the disciple of the Lord" conveyed this information, but since that didn't seem to be enough, he expands the claim beyond John, so that this concept of Jesus' age is claimed to come from "the other apostles also." Irenaeus wrote within a century of John's death, yet does anyone today actually believe that not only John but the rest of the apostles likewise taught their followers that Jesus was in His sixth decade of life when He died? No one believes Irenaeus's arguments, for they are not textually grounded; however, to *not* believe this means either that Irenaeus was lying when he wrote these words or that "oral tradition" can be corrupted *very* quickly.

---

[31]Irenaeus, *Against Heresies*, 2:22:5.

Two lessons can be learned from Irenaeus at this point.

First, in reference to the idea that there is an apostolically originated "rule of faith," the only possible grounds for accepting such a concept would be first to see it as merely a summary statement of apostolic teaching, *and* we would have to obtain this summary from all across the spectrum of early Christian writing, not from any one particular source. This is pretty much what we see; the earliest examples are very basic, very brief, and over time it expands. Obviously, the expansions are subject to suspicion, but we also see a concern that this rule of faith comes from all across the spectrum of ancient churches, not just from a single church or group of churches. The wider the testimony, the more solid is the foundation upon which to rest the rule of faith.

Second, it seems impossible to avoid concluding that if an allegedly apostolic tradition can be corrupted in less than a century, how can we take seriously the claim of Rome that her Marian dogmas, and in particular such beliefs as the Immaculate Conception and the Bodily Assumption—beliefs not even mentioned in their modern form for *centuries* of church history and not dogmatically defined until recent years—are truly apostolic in origin and form? Surely one would have to see such dogmas as divine revelation on the same ground as Scripture to have any meaningful basis for calling them "apostolic."

DEVELOPMENT OF DOCTRINE

Roman Catholicism's most celebrated nineteenth-century convert in the United Kingdom was John Henry Cardinal Newman. A brilliant historian and thinker, Newman's writings have become foundational to many who seek to defend Rome's claims in our era, and he is probably best known for his "development hypothesis."[32] Briefly stated, he argued that Christian truth "develops" in the church's consciousness over time; hence, as the living church reflects upon the divine deposit of faith (contained in the written Scriptures and the unwritten traditions), her understanding of that divine deposit grows.

---

[32]See King and Webster, *Holy Scripture*, 275ff.

This growth results in deeper appreciation of the richness of this truth and the ever-more accurate and full definitions of the truths contained therein.

The analogy of the acorn growing into the full oak tree has often been used to illustrate the concept. This is how Newman explained the lack of historical evidence of a conscious belief in the early centuries in some of the later dogmatic formulations of the Roman Church (papacy, Marian doctrines, etc.). These beliefs were implicitly found in the tradition of that time, but it took more time for the church's reflection to result in the full development of these doctrines in her consciousness, leading to their dogmatic definition.

Frequently, according to Newman, development was prompted not merely by simple questions but by outright heresies, such as that of Arius in the fourth century. Arius denied the deity of Christ, and he began teaching his views to anyone who would listen. Prior to this, no one had been forced to specifically address what Arius was presenting. This does not mean that prior to Arius no one believed in the deity of Christ—they most certainly did—but since it was not the burning issue of the day, exact formulations of the doctrine were not needed. Thus, these more exact formulations that arose to combat heresy were not *new* doctrines or *new* revelations but *developments* and *explanations* of previously held beliefs. Nothing new is added by this clarification process; the foundations were there from the very beginning in God's revelation. But the further *development* of those basic building blocks took time, and for some concepts, especially the Marian doctrines, it took millennia.

This view presented by Newman contains much truth. The example of Arius is excellent, and despite the fact that it's certainly not demonstrable that the church of the days of Athanasius can in any way be said to be identical (or even closely related) to modern Roman Catholicism, it illustrates it accurately. As time has passed, questions have been asked of the Christian faith, which have required answers, and many times those answers have required original thinking upon the once-for-all-delivered-to-the-saints faith of which Jude speaks (Jude 3).

As the gospel moved out into the world, it encountered new cultures and new philosophies. These people asked questions not directly addressed in the Holy Scriptures. For instance, the Greeks asked some questions that are addressed by Paul and some that are not. The early Fathers felt it was appropriate to answer those questions, and they did not feel they had to limit themselves solely to the language of Scripture to do so. When a Greek asked a question couched in Greek philosophical language, men such as Justin Martyr answered the question in Greek philosophical language so that the inquirer could understand the answer. We may (rightly) assert that Justin overstepped and became enamored with Greek philosophy at the expense of biblical revelation, but the point is this: Over the years Christians have thought upon God's revelation and, under the influence of God's Spirit, have gained insight into scriptural truths. *This is the proper development of doctrine.*

Though it may seem surprising to some, in many aspects the Christian scholar of today is "closer" to the original writings of the apostles than people who lived as little as two centuries later. Why? For one thing, we not only have ready access to the entire Bible but also many of the secular writings of the day that give us important historical, cultural, and/or linguistic information. We have the Bible available to us in the original tongues[33] as well as in many excellent translations. We also have access to a vast amount of writing from generations between then and now; we can read the works of men like Spurgeon, Warfield, Hodge, and Machen, and can glean insights unavailable to many over the centuries. While a person living in the sixth century might have been *chronologically* nearer to the time of Paul, he would not have had nearly as much opportunity to *study* the Pauline writings as we have today. We can include in our studies the historical backgrounds of the cities to which Paul was writing; we can read his letters in their original language. These days we can sit at a computer and ask it to provide

---

[33]The vast majority of the early Fathers, for example, were not able to read both Hebrew and Greek, and many in the Western church could not read either one!

us with all the aorist passive participles in his letter to the Romans.[34] These considerations allow us to be far more biblical in our teaching and doctrine than the person who had to live his life in hiding due to persecution, resulting in limited access to the Scriptures and also to those able to teach him.

So Protestants and Catholics agree that doctrine develops, but we strongly disagree about *how* it develops. For Newman, the guiding force in development is the magisterium of the Catholic Church; this can be seen in a quote from Karl Keating, discussing the development of doctrine:

> Consider the doctrine of the Trinity. It is not present on the face of Scripture, not just in the sense that the word Trinity is never used . . . but also in the sense that it is by no means obvious, from the surface meaning of the text, that the Holy Spirit is a divine Person. We naturally read back into the Bible the beliefs we already hold, each of us having been instructed in the faith before picking up the Bible. References to the Holy Spirit's divinity seem to jump out at us. If we imagine ourselves as ancient pagans or as present-day non-Christians coming across the Bible for the first time, we realize that the status of the Holy Spirit is by no means clear. If we think of ourselves as having no recourse to divine Tradition and to the Magisterium of the Church, we can appreciate how easy it must have been for the early pneumatological heresies to arise.[35]

Note very carefully what he says: Regarding the Trinity, allegedly, the doctrine itself is not plain in Scripture. How then do we know about it? Because we are taught it. And who taught it to us? For the Roman Catholic, the magisterium did, through bishops, priests, etc. Though not expressly stated, the conclusion is obvious: The Bible is *unclear* and hence *insufficient* in and of itself to teach the whole truth. Something else is needed— and that something else for the Roman Church is the magisterium and tradition. Keating says this when he writes (in the same chapter cited above) that the trouble with all fundamen-

---

[34]There are eighteen.
[35]Karl Keating, *Catholicism and Fundamentalism* (Ignatius Press, 1988), 144–45.

talists is that they labor "under the misconception that Scripture has the last word and that the Tradition built on oral teaching counts for nothing."[36]

Therefore, what guides "development of doctrine" in Roman Catholicism? It is easy to claim "the Holy Spirit," but in reality the guiding force is the hierarchy of the Church itself. The magisterium claims full interpretive control over the Bible, and, since it is then the "sole guide" to the "development of doctrine," it can steer its own course. Historically, this is just what happened: many doctrinal formulations that Rome claims "developed" over time are not only *non-biblical* but downright *anti-biblical.* These came about as a result of a process; however, it was not *development of Christian doctrine* but *slowly departing from Christian doctrine.*

What then is the correct guiding factor in development? *The guiding factor for the development of Christian doctrine is the Bible itself!* The text of Scripture provides the *grounds* and, most important, the *limits* for this development over time. Rather than bringing in outside influences (such as tradition), we recognize that no one has ever plumbed the depths of God's revelation contained in Scripture; no one has ever come close to exhausting what is to be found in its pages. Therefore, real development of Christian doctrine is simply our ever-increasing understanding of the Word. It is a delving deeper and deeper into the truths of the Word. It involves the recognition of how one passage is related to another, one truth to another. Christian scholars discovering more and more about the biblical languages, the meanings of words, and the forms of expression brings about development of our understanding and, hence, further definition of doctrine. On the spiritual level, it comes about through the Spirit's illumination of those who humbly submit themselves to the Bible's authority, not those who arrogantly assume they have a position of authority *over* the Word.

The example of Arius (cited above) highlights this. Anyone who has read the treatises of Athanasius or Augustine relevant to the Trinity and the deity of Christ knows that these men

---

[36]Ibid., 151.

dealt with Scripture as their source. They exegeted biblical passages, showing how their opponents' position was inconsistent with the entirety of the biblical revelation, and that process has continued to this day.

For example, in the late eighteenth century a man named Granville Sharp formulated a rule of Greek grammar that today bears his name (Greek grammarians are not known for being altogether creative in naming rules). "Granville Sharp's Rule" basically states that if you have two nouns, the first with an article before it and the second without, and they are connected by the word *and,* then both nouns are describing the *same* object. What is the significance? Well, Titus 2:13 contains a "Granville Sharp" construction, and since this rule was recognized as being valid for the Greek language *after* the translation of the King James Version, those translators did not follow the rule and rendered the verse as follows: "Looking for that blessed hope, and the glorious appearing of the great God and our Saviour Jesus Christ." Now, it's not that the translation is *wrong* so much as it's not as *clear* as it could be; in this form one could misconstrue the text to be differentiating between the terms "God" and "Savior." But when Granville Sharp is taken into account, the rendering is clearer: "Looking for the blessed hope and the glorious appearing of our great God and Savior, Christ Jesus." Therefore, the recognition of this standard has increased our understanding of the doctrine of the deity of Jesus Christ, for here Paul uses the term *God* of the Lord Jesus. This is biblically based doctrinal development guided not by a group of men claiming apostolic authority but by the text of Scripture itself.

Another example is found in the meaning of the Greek word *monogenes,* traditionally translated "only begotten." Many non-Christian groups have attempted to deny the eternal nature of Christ on the basis of this term, misunderstanding the term *begotten* and asserting some point of beginning for the second person of the Trinity. Yet by studying papyri found in the Egyptian deserts within the last century, scholars have realized that an error was made in earlier understandings of this word. It was assumed that the term was made up of two parts: *monos,* which means "only," and *gennao,* which is a verb meaning "to beget, give birth to."

The assumption was half correct. *Monogenes* does come from *monos* but not from *gennao;* rather, the second part of the word comes from a noun, *genos,* that means "kind" or "type." Therefore, *monogenes* means "one of a kind, unique" rather than "only begotten," and, accordingly, the term was used of an only son, a unique son. The importance for Christology is clear: No one can base a denial of the Son's eternal nature upon this term, for it does not refer to a "beginning" at all but instead describes the uniqueness of its object.

Both our examples so far have been based upon linguistic studies; another example is the atonement of Christ. History tells us that the early Fathers had some interesting views of the Atonement; that hardly one agreed with another on the subject. Their writings on the matter, however, show a great lack of clarity on the whole council of God and consistent in-depth exegesis of the relevant passages is lacking in many patristic sources. Part of this may be due to the extensive time and energy that was put into the doctrine of Christ's *person* rather than His *work* at an early stage. Whatever the reason, some very *unbiblical* doctrines regarding the nature of the Atonement have been popular in the past and continue to this day. Even so, as believers committed solely to the authority of God's Word have studied the Bible's teaching on the subject, many of the false impressions prevalent in the past have been put aside, and the truth of Christ's atoning work is much more readily available to someone today than only four centuries ago. This, again, is *development.* It is not change, for the limitations of the proper use of development are set by the very words of Scripture itself. It is not an imposition of external concepts or authorities upon the teaching of the Bible (as we see in Roman Catholic doctrine). Rather, it is a digging ever more deeply into the revelation of God, a prayerful seeking of His guidance and direction.

Once again, we cannot overemphasize the importance of doctrinal development's *guiding principle.* In Catholicism, the guiding principle is the Church itself—what else could it be? Catholic leaders tell us the Bible is not a safe guide and is not complete in and of itself. Sacred tradition must be allowed to speak as well, and who does tradition use to speak but the magisterium of Rome? How then could the Bible itself define the boundaries of development if it is not a complete, sufficient revelation? From Rome's perspective, given what she teaches about the Bible, the Christian concept of a biblically defined realm of doctrinal development is not logical or possible, but when we reject Rome's concept of revelation and her claims over the interpretation of Scripture, the concept of a continuing process of study and enlightenment based upon God's Word is not only logical but also beautiful.

Nevertheless, has not study of the Bible also led to an abandonment of some of the faith's central doctrines in recent centuries? Do we not see "Christian" scholars who, on the basis of modern theories of how the Bible was written, or of the Bible's nature, jettison such teachings as original sin, God's providence, the Trinity, and the resurrection of the dead? We do see many who claim to be Christians rejecting biblical truth on the basis of unproven and unprovable theories about Scripture. The notion that the Bible is but a collection of myths and legends *is* common today, but this is not real biblical study. These people do not allow the Word to speak for itself. They reject the supernatural worldview of the Bible and impose their own anti-supernatural concepts upon it. We have asserted that true doctrinal development comes when Christians committed to the absolute authority of the Scriptures are guided in their studies by the Spirit of God. We have already discussed how central one's view of the nature of Scripture (inerrancy and inspired internal coherence) is to the process of interpretation. While such unbelieving "biblical scholars" may even appear at times to be in the majority, *God's purposes will not fail.*

In conclusion, we see that when Roman apologists use the concept of "doctrinal development" as a defense for the various teachings of Rome, they are wrongly using a right principle. One cannot speak of doctrinal *development* when attempting to defend the cult of Mary or the concept of papal infallibility.

These ideas are not only missing from Scripture but are also anti-scriptural to the core. They are not developments based upon further biblical study, but departures based upon exterior sources of authority. *True development is based upon the obedient study of the God-breathed Scriptures, where the Holy Spirit blesses that study with greater insights into the depths of the revelation contained therein.*

CHAPTER 10

The Lord Spoke to Me, Saying...

GEORGE: It was just fantastic, Josh. I really hadn't known what to do, so I opened my Bible to the Psalms and started reading. And right then, God spoke to me. He told me to buy the *Deep Spirit Study Bible* in teal and genuine leather! It cost an arm and a leg, but I'm sure the Lord will provide.

JOSHUA: Let me see if I understand you, George: God spoke to you in an audible voice?

GEORGE: Joshua, I know you have a problem with walking in the Spirit and all, but this is part of my regular life! It wasn't an audible voice. I mean, you wouldn't have heard it if you'd been sitting next to me.

JOSHUA: So it was a voice inside your head, or an impression?

GEORGE: Well, I'd been praying about it, and as I started to meditate on the Word, I received confirmation that that was what I should do.

JOSHUA: What in the text told you that?

GEORGE: Oh no, it wasn't the text. It was just while I was reading that I was thinking about it, and then I got this feeling—which is sort of hard to explain—but a warm feeling, and I *knew* I was to get that Bible. I know I'll learn a lot from it.

JOSHUA: Okay, so there was nothing in the inspired text that told you what you should do. You had been looking at that leather Bible, almost purchased it, then couldn't get it out of your mind. And as you sat down with your old Bible and opened it up, all of a sudden you felt like you should go and buy the one you had seen. Right?

GEORGE: Joshua, Joshua. You need to listen to some of the phenomenal Christian leaders today who are really in tune with the Spirit and who could teach you to likewise experience the Spirit's leadership and guidance.

JOSHUA: I'm doing just fine with the elders the Lord has given me, thank you. However, I'm trying to understand you here. Remember last week when the Mormons came by your home and we talked about how to respond to them?

GEORGE: Sure. They had the *Book of Mormon* and *Doctrine and Covenants* and . . . something else.

JOSHUA: *The Pearl of Great Price.*

GEORGE: Right.

JOSHUA: And remember how we talked about *sola scriptura* and the sufficiency of the Bible to act as the sole rule of faith for the church over against the denial of that belief by Mormons, Catholics, and many other groups?

GEORGE: Sure. And I agreed with you that the Bible is what we need. The Spirit never contradicts the Bible, and we believe the Bible alone.

JOSHUA: Right. Well, that's what is giving me problems here. See, on the one hand you said you believed special revelation in the form of Scripture was completed and fully represented by the Bible, so that we did not need Joseph Smith's additional "scriptures," or the "traditions" of Rome, or even the "faithful and discreet slave" of the Watchtower. [1]

GEORGE: Of course. All we need is the Bible.

---

[1] Watchtower Bible and Tract Society, Jehovah's Witnesses.

JOSHUA: Yet you started this conversation by talking about what God *said* to you.

GEORGE: Oh, well, come on, Josh . . . I don't mean what He says to me is on the same level as Scripture!

JOSHUA: When Isaiah said, "The Lord spoke to me, saying," what followed was Scripture, wasn't it?

GEORGE: Yeah, but I'm not a prophet.

JOSHUA: So when the Spirit spoke to you and told you to buy that Bible, this was some kind of secondary revelation, not scriptural, but still the Spirit speaking with that level of clarity?

GEORGE: It was an impression—you know, a spiritual feeling.

JOSHUA: Yes, I know what a spiritual feeling is like. I remember once when witnessing to a Mormon I felt strongly constrained to talk to him about a topic I almost never talk about when witnessing to Mormons, and, in fact, had not even thought about that day. As it turned out, this was the *exact* topic that would open him to a discussion of the gospel. But I would never say, "God spoke to me and said such and such," and, what is more, there was nothing in my spiritual impression that could be construed as carrying "revelatory information" or the like.

GEORGE: Well, you can relax, because I am not claiming to be getting any new Scriptures.

JOSHUA: I know, but I'm still confused. First you said you believe in *sola scriptura,* but when I asked you what in the text was used by the Spirit to give you understanding, you said there was no connection between the actual words of the text and what you decided to do. Hence, you seem to be saying the Spirit was giving specific directions totally apart from the Word of God.

GEORGE: But you said you once had such an impression too.

JOSHUA: Ah, but I was ministering the Word of God, had started the conversation, and had a number of directions I could go—all sound biblical routes designed to share the truth of the gospel with that Mormon fellow. The Spirit simply brought to my mind a divine truth, one of many denied by Mormonism, and directed my thinking thereto. I had to have already studied the relevant issues, memorized the relevant passages, etc., and I had to know, from the Bible, the truths to share with him once the conversation moved in that direction. I would be violating *sola scriptura* if I said to you, "I had never once talked about this issue, and I knew nothing about it, and God just zapped me with this mountain of information I'd never thought of before."

GEORGE: I can see that, I guess. I hadn't considered that difference before. But still, don't you believe the Spirit speaks today? I mean, at my church, He speaks every worship service!

JOSHUA: Is this speaking on the same level of Scripture?

GEORGE: Of course not. We test it by Scripture.

JOSHUA: So is what the Spirit says infallible?

GEORGE: Well, only when speaking in Scripture.

JOSHUA: When someone says something that is clearly wrong but says the Spirit told him to say it, what do you do?

GEORGE: Well, we realize that sometimes people are just confusing their own wants and desires with the Spirit's voice. That's why we need Scripture.

JOSHUA: And how do you employ Scripture to test something like buying a leather teal-colored study Bible?

GEORGE: Heh, good question. I guess you don't, outside of making sure it isn't sinful or something like that.

JOSHUA: George, just how possible is it that you had a very strong desire to buy the Bible, overcame all other objections, decided to do so, and felt good about it, but that the Spirit did not "say" anything about it at all? How would you know otherwise?

GEORGE: It's something you learn when you get deep into the Spirit, Josh. Just something you get hold of.

JOSHUA: Okay, well, when you talked to those Mormons, didn't they say they had a testimony given to them by the Spirit?

GEORGE: They did, yeah. That sort of surprised me.

JOSHUA: Didn't surprise me at all. I've talked to many fine LDS folks, and the claim to a Spirit-borne testimony is common among them. As I recall, you had no problem with the means I suggested for dealing with their claimed testimony.

GEORGE: Yep, you said their feelings have to be tested by Scripture, and if they contradict, then they can't come from the Holy Spirit, because that would cause contradiction between the author of Scripture and Scripture itself.

JOSHUA: Right. Now, you'd admit the Bible nowhere says the *Book of Mormon,* for example, is *not* God's Word, since the *Book of Mormon* did not exist when the Bible was written. So how can we test a Mormon's claim that the Spirit tells him the *Book of Mormon* is the Word of God?

GEORGE: I guess by comparing the teachings of the *Book of Mormon* with the Bible.

JOSHUA: Exactly. But this means we have to subject these "spiritual feelings" to an objective standard, correct?

GEORGE: Oh yes, I agree completely.

JOSHUA: Without meaning to offend, then, are you really consistent here in your practice?

GEORGE: What do you mean?

JOSHUA: Well, your favorite evangelist and faith healer was on TV last night; I caught some of his preaching and was pretty amazed at what I heard. He was talking about revelation knowledge, conversations with God, and all sorts of things that you could never test by Scripture. He made claims that I could not honestly differentiate from the kind of miraculous claims made by the apostles. But what *really* caught my attention were his claims regarding the Spirit "teaching" him what the Bible meant in this passage and that.

GEORGE: I bet you disagreed with his interpretations.

JOSHUA: Goodness, yes, but if you believe what the man says, to disagree with him is to disagree with the Holy Spirit Himself. Let me give you an example from last night. He had thousands of men standing in front of him, and he truly had their complete attention—he was quite the orator. But he would pepper his comments with claims that the Spirit was leading, the Spirit was giving him insight, and so on.

GEORGE: Yes, the anointing does that.

JOSHUA: Well, he then cited 1 John 3:2, which reads, "Beloved, now we are children of God, and it has not appeared as yet what we will be. We know that when He appears, we will be like Him, because we will see Him just as He is." Then he told the gathered crowd that the Lord had spoken to him and "revealed" to him that the word *will* was not "in the Greek," and it really meant that "we be like Him," that is, right now, present tense—we are *already* in that state. He went on to insist that this was the way we could have "victory" over all our difficulties: by realizing what we already are.

Now, the fact is, the word *will* represents the verb tense in this passage; John said "we will be like Him" using a future-tense verb in reference to the someday event of Christ's appearing. The Holy Spirit inspired the writing of that future tense verb; hence, the word *will is* there, and the Spirit did *not* tell that evangelist it shouldn't be there. Now, do you test him in the same way, comparing what he says to what's actually there in the text?

GEORGE: I admit that most of the time I don't check everything out, unless it sounds really strange. . . .

JOSHUA: Honestly, I didn't see a single open Bible in the audience, and I heard no one objecting. How about you? I know you respect this man greatly, but this was hardly the first time I've seen him engage in this kind of activity.

GEORGE: Josh, I really am uncomfortable questioning God's anointing on a person's life. I mean, look at how many people have been saved through his ministry!

JOSHUA: The old pragmatic approach: If you see what you deem to be good results, it must mean the Spirit is involved.

GEORGE: What else can explain it? He has thirteen thousand people in his church today, and he started out a few years ago with only a few hundred!

JOSHUA: Joseph Smith's religion started with six people in 1830, and today there are twelve million. Mohammed started with no one, and now there are a billion Muslims in the world. Contrast that with Jesus, who had five thousand men listening to Him on one day, and by the end of the next only twelve confused men remained, one of whom He said was a devil. Truth is never determined by numbers or popularity.

The fact remains: The Spirit never said what the

evangelist *claimed* the Spirit said. That is a fact, for it would contradict Spirit-inspired Scripture. If, when we can actually check the facts of what he says, he is wrong, how then can we blindly accept those instances where we have no means of checking his claims? Do you simply accept the words of anyone who claims "the anointing"?

GEORGE: No way. I test the spirits, as the Bible says.

JOSHUA: Irony of ironies, that comes from 1 John, the same book this man misrepresented, so by what standard do you test the spirits, when your favorite evangelist can change the very text of the same book? What if he told you the Spirit assured him that it doesn't really say "test the spirits" but rather "support those who are spiritual"—would you go along with him?

GEORGE: I honestly haven't thought about it.

JOSHUA: I would hope you'd reject such a claim immediately and realize that no "anointing" gives anyone the right to alter the text of Scripture—which sort of takes us back around to your original situation.

GEORGE: I don't claim *that* kind of anointing!

JOSHUA: I didn't know there was a graduated scale of anointing for such things, but I think your response does reveal something. You recognize that there is a relationship between what you claim regarding the Spirit "speaking" to you about "little things"—like buying your new Bible—and the same Spirit allegedly telling your favorite teacher something directly contrary to the text of Scripture.

GEORGE: Okay, so let me turn this around. You believe in the Holy Spirit?

JOSHUA: Of course. The Holy Spirit is fully divine, eternal, omnipotent, and the other "Comforter" [2] Jesus promised His people. It is through the Spirit's presence in the life of His people that Christ's presence is made real in their experience. [3] Yes, I believe in the Holy Spirit.

GEORGE: So how is the Spirit active in your life?

JOSHUA: In my church we often confess in our prayers that

---

[2]Or "Advocate," or "Helper." See John 14:26; 15:26; 16:7.
[3]See John 14:23.

"apart from your Spirit, we can do nothing." We pray God's Spirit will open our eyes to the truth of His Word and create in us a clean heart zealous for good deeds and longing to be obedient to Him. On a daily basis the Spirit convicts me of sin, gives me wisdom, and, when I'm studying the Scriptures, opens up my understanding so that I may see wonderful things in His Word.

GEORGE: Fine, but *how* does the Spirit guide you? Does He speak to you?

JOSHUA: Not in the sense you're promoting, George, no. I believe the Spirit and the Word cannot be separated in that way. I believe the normative ministry of the Spirit is to use the means God has given us through the church to grow us in the grace and knowledge of the Lord Jesus Christ.

GEORGE: Why do you say "normative"?

JOSHUA: Because in many of these conversations the unusual and the extreme is made the norm. I am often asked, "Well, couldn't God do some miracle like this?" as if the more unlikely and odd something is, the more important it is to the normal Christian life. When I look at God's Word I see the church with elders and deacons, meeting on the Lord's Day, singing psalms and hymns, praying, reading the Word, and being instructed from the Scriptures. I see the church baptizing, teaching, and engaging in the Lord's Supper. The Spirit is actively involved in all of these things, again, using them to grow us in the grace and knowledge of our Lord Jesus Christ.

GEORGE: When the Spirit works in you, *how does this happen?*

JOSHUA: In my experience, He uses the Scriptures either directly, in the form of those passages I have memorized or become very familiar with, or, more indirectly, by bringing scriptural themes, concepts, and guidelines to my mind. In this way I am able to grow in godly wisdom, make godly decisions, learn to avoid sin, and in general glorify my heavenly Father by living as a Christian grounded firmly in His Word. The Spirit is the one who does all of this.

GEORGE: That's it?

JOSHUA: *It?* Believe me, it takes a pretty special miracle to get spiritual truth through my thick skull! I know it's not the kind of miracle that would get aired on "Christian television," but yes, I think it's downright miraculous how the Spirit works in concert with the Word in the believer's life. I mean, He takes an inspired, inerrant Scripture, preserves it over time, raises me to spiritual life, gives me a nature that longs for His truth and His Word, draws me to it, sheds His light upon it, teaches me through its words and precepts, writes its truths upon my heart, and then brings those truths to my mind when I need His wisdom. If that's not one amazing set of miracles, I don't know what is.

But you know, George, one of the reasons people underestimate just how tremendously special the ministry of the Spirit is in doing all those things is that the only way anyone else can *see* that work is over the long haul. Growth takes time; increasing in wisdom, learning the Word, experiencing sanctification . . . all of that can only be seen in hindsight over a long period. We live in an age of instant gratification, so the Spirit has been molded to fit what *we* want. But I truly believe that the only real and sound evidence of the Spirit's activity is not in the flashy short-run claims of spiritual experiences but in the long run, "made it through the daily grind for thirty years and remained faithful despite a million obstacles" kind of life that endures to the end and glorifies God.

GEORGE: That sure sounds biblical, Josh, but let's bring it full circle: How do you decide what kind of Bible to buy, if not by the Spirit?

JOSHUA: I believe the Spirit builds Christian character over time through the ministry of the Word and personal sanctification. If I apply godly principles to my everyday living, I will seek to make decisions and choices that honor my heavenly Father and my Lord Jesus Christ. Thus I would seek to purchase a Bible that would be most useful to me over time—which, unfortunately, would probably exclude most current Study Bibles. I would seek to purchase one that would be long-lasting, easy for my aging eyes to read, and within my financial means without restricting my ability to help others. I would say this is the normative way in which

God would guide His people in their everyday behavior. However, to really bring this full circle, let me come back to the issue of *sola scriptura*. George, if Scripture truly is the sole infallible rule of faith for the church, and if it provides you with all that you need for life and godliness, [4] do you see how the uncritical use of the phrase "The Lord spoke to me, saying . . ." at best could be seen as inconsistent?

GEORGE: Well, like I said, I'm not claiming to receive Scripture. . . .

JOSHUA: True, but have you given sufficient serious thought to just what is the nature of this not-quite-Scripture-but-still-a-form-of-divine-revelation? For many, questioning this usage is tantamount to saying the Spirit has retired from the world, but as I have proved, this is not the case at all. The issue really is, "What is the nature of the Spirit's ministry in the church over time?"

GEORGE: I'll give it some thought. I certainly don't want to believe anything other than what the Spirit Himself has inspired, and I saw from talking to the Mormons that you need a firm foundation upon which to stand to confront false teachings. My emotions are *not* that firm foundation.

---

[4] 2 Peter 1:3.

CHAPTER 11

Scriptural Sufficiency: Nothing New

ROBERT: The final proof of your error, Joshua, is this: No one believed what you believe about the sufficiency of Scripture *until the Reformation*. How could all of the earliest generations have missed such an obvious truth if it was what the apostles intended their followers to believe?

JOSHUA: A very common assertion, Robert—I've spoken with many people who have honestly believed what you just said. And I can understand why, if all you've ever heard has been the repeated mantra that the early church was the equivalent of the modern Vatican without cell phones. Since church history is a subject many evangelicals ignore completely—much to their detriment—perhaps you have not spoken with many who could offer a substantive response. In fact, in my experience, there is an automatic presumption that if someone seeks to point to early writers who did not hold to specifically Roman Catholic viewpoints, then they must be mishandling or misrepresenting those authors.

ROBERT: That Protestants generally ignore church history is testimony of church history's Catholic nature.

JOSHUA: Not necessarily. Their works may not be at the top of the bestseller lists, but non-Catholic scholars have interacted extensively with early church writings on this and many such subjects. [1]

ROBERT: So you read the writings of the Fathers?

JOSHUA: Not as a regular aspect of my devotional life, no, but I find the writings of the early church to be useful in understanding the faith's development. Some of their writings, like the Epistles of Ignatius or the Epistle to Diognetus, are tremendously encouraging; others are less so, since there have been untaught and unstable men throughout church history, many of whom have decided to write. Anyway, these uninspired writings, while at times encouraging, insightful, and useful, are at other times reflective of unbiblical and inferior theology. Each writer, and each book written by each author, must be evaluated by the standard of Scripture, just as we do with modern authors.

ROBERT: Then you don't believe the Fathers were the containers of the oral tradition passed down from the apostles?

JOSHUA: No, and I don't think they viewed themselves that way—do you? That seems to be a rather anachronistic way of considering them. In fact, that's one of my main problems with how people look at those early writers: We ask questions of them that they had no intention of answering. We need to let them speak in their own context. If they weren't even thinking about our modern controversies, why are we trying to drag them into our battles? Which brings us back to your original assertion: You seem to think that viewing the Bible as a sufficient source of knowledge of God's truth without the addition of external sources of revelation or infallible authority was unknown to the early church.

ROBERT: Correct. They knew the need for tradition.

JOSHUA: Well, let's be fair to them: They were not debating

---

[1] Again, I strongly encourage you to see the work of David King and William Webster, *Holy Scripture: The Ground and Pillar of Our Faith,* for the best contemporary representation of such materials and for a significantly fuller list of relevant patristic citations.

what we're debating today. Requiring that they use the same terms and address the same issues we face and disagree about today would be unfair.

ROBERT: You don't believe we can learn anything from the early Fathers about their view of authority?

JOSHUA: Don't misunderstand me; we can learn much. But remember two important facts: First, the writings of those early believers are not inspired; second, what they say about anything, including authority, Scripture, or tradition, cannot be elevated to the position of divine revelation.

ROBERT: But what they said about tradition . . .

JOSHUA: You mean like what Irenaeus[2] said?

> To which course many nations of those barbarians who believe in Christ do assent, having salvation written in their hearts by the Spirit, without paper or ink, and carefully preserving the ancient tradition, believing in one God, the Creator of heaven and earth, and all things therein, by means of Christ Jesus, the Son of God.[3]

Notice, Robert, that the "ancient tradition" of Irenaeus is defined as *a belief in one God, and the role of Christ as the Creator.* Likewise, he said,

> We have learned from none others [the apostles] the plan of our salvation, than from those through whom the Gospel has come down to us, which they did at one time proclaim in public, and, at a later period, by the will of God, handed down to us in the Scriptures, to be the ground and pillar of our faith. . . . These have all declared to us that there is one God, Creator of heaven and earth, announced by the law and the prophets; and one Christ, the Son of God. If any one do not agree to these truths, he despises the companions of the Lord; nay more, he despises Christ Himself the Lord; yea, he despises the Father also, and stands self-condemned, resisting

---

[2]Irenaeus lived c. 130–c. 200.

[3]*Against Heresies*, III:4:2. References in this chapter will be to the titled works rather than to various translations of them; most of these citations are available in standard collections or online. The tradition of Irenaeus is clearly and fully laid out in I:10:1, replete with direct citations of Scripture.

and opposing his own salvation, as is the case with all heretics. [4]

ROBERT: Well, he was dealing with one particular issue, so he emphasized one aspect of that tradition. That doesn't mean there were no other aspects.

JOSHUA: Okay, let's grant that assumption. The point is, one of the earliest definitions of "ancient tradition" was limited to truths that are clearly taught in Scripture. This "tradition" of Irenaeus, which he claimed was found throughout the true churches, is not some extra-biblical concept but is a summary of Scripture's basic teachings. Nothing here substantiates the idea that the Bible *without* this tradition is somehow incomplete; the point is, there's a basic thrust and foundation to biblical revelation, and if you start off without that foundation you will make a mess of your reading of the Scriptures. For example, Mormons start off with belief in a plurality of gods, derived from their other works of "scripture," and thus end up completely missing the most basic biblical truths. The same was true in Irenaeus's day: The gnostics began with a false assumption and then read it into the Bible.

ROBERT: But tradition is a much wider concept than that. The early church depended upon tradition for its knowledge of God and proper worship.

JOSHUA: Hippolytus [5] seemingly had a different view:

> There is, brethren, one God, the knowledge of whom we gain from the Holy Scriptures, and from no other source. . . . Whatever things, then, the Holy Scriptures declare, at these let us look; and whatsoever things they teach, these let us learn. [6]

But Robert, if we want to look to someone who really illustrated what it means to stand for the truth about the nature of God, and especially in reference to the deity of Christ, we

---

[4] Ibid., III:1:1–2. It is important to point out why Irenaeus was so concerned about the "tradition" teaching that there is one God who created all things by Jesus Christ. He was struggling against gnosticism, a system denying that the one true God created all things; again, the gnostics posited intermediate beings between the one true God and the creation.

[5] Hippolytus lived c. 170–c. 236.

[6] *Against the Heresy of One Noetus*, 9.

can look to Athanasius.[7] Here was a man whose staunch
and unflinching defense of orthodoxy, even in the face of
the defection of the *vast* majority of the professing church
of his day, prompted the saying *Athanasius contra mundum*,
"Athanasius against the world." His tenacious unwillingness
to give in on the key issue of the nature of Christ produced
one of the most important writing periods in church history. Yet his work is filled with statements that sound dissim-
ilar to what you're saying the early church was like when it
comes to authority and Scripture. For instance, "The tokens
of truth are more exact as drawn from Scripture, than from
other sources."[8]

ROBERT: But that doesn't mean Scripture is the *only* source.

JOSHUA: Agreed, but please note, if there *is* some other source,
it is *less exact* in the definition of truth, which would indicate
its *inferiority* to the Scriptures. Beyond this, this statement
was made in reference to those who were seeking to overthrow the Nicene definition. Amazing, isn't it, that in this
context Athanasius would say those words? There are also
others, such as, "Vainly then do they run about with the
pretext that they have demanded Councils for the faith's
sake; for divine Scripture is sufficient above all things"[9] and
"The sacred and inspired Scriptures are sufficient to
declare the truth."[10]

ROBERT: No one has ever said the early writers did not honor
the Scriptures just as we do today.

JOSHUA: Indeed, but these statements do not sound much like
those who today go about denying *sola scriptura*, do they?
When Athanasius wrote his Festal Letter he listed the
canon—excluding the freestanding books of the Apocrypha, by the way—and then said:

> These are fountains of salvation, that they who thirst may
> be satisfied with the living words they contain. In these alone

---

[7]Athanasius lived c. 297–373 and was bishop of Alexandria.
[8]*De Decretis*, 7.
[9]*History of Councils*, 6.
[10]*Against the Heathen*, 1:1.

is proclaimed the doctrine of godliness. Let no man add to these, neither let him take ought from these. For concerning these the Lord put to shame the Sadducees, and said, "Ye do err, not knowing the Scriptures." And He reproved the Jews, saying, "Search the Scriptures, for these are they that testify of Me."[11]

These *alone,* Robert? Isn't oral tradition also a fountain of salvation? Isn't the doctrine of godliness proclaimed in "tradition"? See, you can't define your modern views of tradition in the same terms used in these early documents.

ROBERT: Athanasius did, however, refer to "apostolic tradition."

JOSHUA: Yes, he did; for example, in his letter to Adelphius he makes reference to apostolic tradition by saying, "While the Apostolic tradition teaches in the words of blessed Peter, 'Forasmuch then as Christ suffered for us in the Flesh,' and in what Paul writes, 'Looking for the blessed hope and appearing of our great God and Savior Jesus Christ. . . .'"[12] Do you see what he was doing? This "apostolic tradition" is nothing other than the Scriptures themselves. You would be very hard pressed, in looking at all of his writings, to develop the idea that he believed in a separate apostolic tradition being passed down outside of the Word, to be held in equal authority with the God-breathed Scriptures.

ROBERT: Even if that was true, Athanasius is just one theologian, one writer—

JOSHUA: That can be said of anyone, such as Cyril of Jerusalem.[13] His *Catechetical Lectures* are the words of just one man, but they reflect what was being taught as Christian doctrine in his area at one particular point in time.

ROBERT: You don't want to go there with Cyril. He believed things I know you do not.

JOSHUA: Just the opposite, Robert, for while I agree with you that he did, remember that I do not have to believe every

---

[11] 39th Festal Letter, A.D. 367.
[12] *Letter 60, To Adelphius,* 6.
[13] Cyril lived c. 318–386.

word spoken by every early writer. In fact, Cyril *commanded* his readers to do with his teaching what I do with everyone's:

> Concerning the divine and holy mysteries of the Faith, not even a casual statement must be delivered without the Holy Scriptures; nor must we be drawn aside by mere plausibility and artifices of speech. Even to me, who tell you these things, give not absolute credence, unless you receive the proof of the things which I announce from the Divine Scriptures. For this salvation which we believe depends not on ingenious reasoning, but on demonstration of the Holy Scriptures.[14]

I'm not sure how much more strongly it can be expressed than that, except perhaps in these words:

> Why then do you busy yourself about things which not even the Holy Ghost has written in the Scriptures? You who do not know the things which are written, do you busy yourself about the things which are not written? There are many questions in the Divine Scriptures; what is written we comprehend not, why do we busy ourselves about what is not written? It is sufficient for us to know that God hath begotten One Only Son.[15]

Or these words, which so clearly confirm the divine nature of Scripture and their role in Cyril's view of ultimate authority and divine revelation:

> Let us then speak concerning the Holy Ghost nothing but what is written; and whatsoever is not written, let us not busy ourselves about it. The Holy Ghost Himself spoke the Scriptures; He has also spoken concerning Himself as much as He pleased, or as much as we could receive. Let us therefore speak those things which He has said; for whatsoever He has not said, we dare not say.[16]

Indeed, this seems consistent with the view of Gregory of Nyssa,[17] who wrote,

> We make the Holy Scriptures the canon and the rule of

---

[14]*Catechetical Lectures*, IV:17.
[15]Ibid., XI:12.
[16]Ibid., XVI:2.
[17]Gregory lived c. 335–395.

every dogma; we of necessity look upon that, and receive alone that which may be made conformable to the intention of those writings.[18]

ROBERT: "Made conformable" and "being the only infallible source" are not the same.

JOSHUA: Possibly not, but he had just stated that the Holy Scriptures are the "canon and rule" of *every* dogma. For Gregory, the yardstick is Scripture, is it not?

ROBERT: Yes, I can live with that.

JOSHUA: Great. Let's also look at a few quotes from Basil of Caesaria.[19] This is one of my favorites:

> We ought carefully to examine whether the doctrine offered us is conformable to Scripture, and if not, to reject it. Nothing must be added to the inspired words of God; all that is outside Scripture is not of faith, but is sin.[20]

What do you think Basil meant by "all that is outside Scripture," Robert?

ROBERT: Well, Joshua, one can hold to what is called the *material* sufficiency of Scripture, believing that everything God has revealed and that is necessary is *implicitly* contained in Scripture, even if the Bible is not *formally* sufficient.

JOSHUA: Yes, so I understand. But Basil did not say, "What is outside Scripture might be found implicitly inside Scripture, if we read Scripture from a perspective that will not develop for another one thousand years." Besides, how could anyone do as Basil said and examine a doctrine that claims to be in tradition if one must embrace tradition to properly interpret the Bible? I just don't see how your system can possibly fly here, Robert. The whole idea of our responsibility, based upon knowing and understanding the Scriptures, does not work when you embrace Rome's concept of ultimate and infallible authority. Consider another citation from Basil:

---

[18] *On the Soul and Resurrection.*
[19] Basil lived c. 329–379.
[20] *Prolegomena*, 2, Work 3, Ascetic (iii).

> Concerning the Hearers: that those hearers who are instructed in the Scriptures should examine what is said by the teachers, receiving what is in conformity with the Scriptures and rejecting what is opposed to them; and that those who persist in teaching such doctrines should be strictly avoided.[21]

This again emphasizes the personal responsibility of the hearer to test the teachers by what is in Scripture. Isn't this the very activity you find inconsistent in non-Catholic use of the Bible as the sole infallible and sufficient rule of faith?

ROBERT: Rome does not teach anything contrary to the Scriptures, so that would hardly be relevant to my beliefs.

JOSHUA: Yet when I *do* find doctrines and teachings contrary to the Scriptures being taught by Rome, you say I do not have the right to test those beliefs since they are defined by the infallible magisterium, and that I am engaging in mere "private interpretation." I do not see how that fits with Basil's words. Here's another quote from him:

> To a widow. Enjoying as you do the consolation of the Holy Scriptures, you stand in need neither of my assistance nor of that of anybody else to help you to comprehend your duty. You have the all-sufficient counsel and guidance of the Holy Spirit to lead you to what is right.[22]

From my reading, the more solid, biblically literate, consistent writers in the church's early centuries regularly made this kind of statement about the Scriptures, but they did *not* make the same kind of statement about tradition, or, if they spoke of tradition, they did so either as we saw in the words of Athanasius, defining "apostolic tradition" as the content of Scripture itself or as referring to the practice of ecclesiastical traditions in the church. Basil also did this, speaking of apostolic traditions relating to baptizing and various ceremonies and the like.[23]

Well, seeing we have moved a good distance down through church history and have only touched upon some

---

[21] *The Morals*, Rule 72.
[22] *Letter 283*.
[23] See his *On the Spirit*, 66, for a good example of this.

highlights, we must make sure to include the testimony of Augustine.[24]

ROBERT: A true Catholic bishop.

JOSHUA: Yes, though that meant for him something *very* different than "Roman Catholic," I assure you. But let's examine his vitae: Anyone familiar with church history knows that no man has influenced the course of Christianity more deeply than Augustine, the great North African theologian in the waning days of the Roman empire. Few theologians have left a wider, deeper mark on succeeding generations than Augustine, both for good and for ill. His devotional works still rank among the classics. His theological works cast their shadow across the next fifteen hundred years of theological development. His writings on the church, formed during his controversy with the Donatists in North Africa, laid the very foundation of the later union of church and state and the sacral system of the papacy.[25]

ROBERT: I'm amazed you would admit that, Joshua.

JOSHUA: One need not "admit" history, Robert. But remember, Augustine's writings on grace and salvation would find their clearest expressions *one thousand years later.* That's why both sides of the Reformation were able to quote Augustine, usually with honesty. But his view of authority, and especially of biblical centrality, is well known; few early writers can give us as strong and clear a testimony to their belief in this area. In fact, one of his works, *On the Unity of the Church,* lives and breathes the centrality *and* sufficiency of the Scriptures. I note these selections from that work:

> Let us not hear: This I say, this you say; but, thus says the Lord. Surely it is the books of the Lord on whose authority we both agree and which we both believe. There let us seek the church, there let us discuss our case.... Let those things be removed from our midst which we quote against each other not from divine canonical books but from elsewhere. Someone may perhaps ask: Why do you want to remove these things

---

[24]Aurelius Augustine, the renowned bishop of Hippo, lived c. 354–430.
[25]Note that Augustine himself did not foresee these developments.

from the midst? Because I do not want the holy church proved by human documents but by divine oracles. . . . Whatever they may adduce, and wherever they may quote from, let us rather, if we are His sheep, hear the voice of our Shepherd. Therefore let us search for the church in the sacred canonical Scriptures. . . . Neither dare one agree with catholic bishops if by chance they err in anything, with the result that their opinion is against the canonical Scriptures of God.[26]

ROBERT: But Augustine can't mean what you think he means, since he believed so many things contrary to your beliefs.

JOSHUA: Though that is the common response I receive, it does not follow. His point is clear: the Scriptures are God's divine Word, and we are looking in the wrong place when we seek certainty and sufficiency anywhere else. Augustine obviously didn't hold to a modern Roman Catholic view of authority:

> I must not press the authority of Nicea against you, nor you that of Ariminum against me; I do not acknowledge the one, as you do not the other; but let us come to ground that is common to both—the testimony of the Holy Scriptures.[27]

ROBERT: Well, that's because he was dealing with a heretic who didn't accept tradition anyway.

JOSHUA: So Nicea's authority as an ecclesiastical council *does* differ in nature from that of Scripture? Doesn't it tell you something that one can be unbound to a council's authority but still be bound to that of Scripture? Here's another:

> What more shall I teach you than what we read in the apostle? For Holy Scripture fixes the rule for our doctrine, lest we dare to be wiser than we ought. Therefore I should not teach you anything else except to expound to you the words of the Teacher.[28]

Can you honestly say, Robert, that Holy Scripture fixes the rule of your doctrine, or does the magisterium have the final say in that matter?

---

[26] *De unitate ecclesiae*, 10.
[27] *To Maximin the Arian.*
[28] *De bono viduitatis*, 2.

ROBERT: Holy Scripture is vital and in fact central to the definition of what we believe; for many things, yes, it is the standard, but not the *only* standard.

JOSHUA: But Augustine said he would not teach anything else except to expound the word of the Teacher, which he found in the Holy Scriptures. When you are teaching any one of your numerous dogmas that have been defined in the many centuries since Augustine, are you not thereby saying he was wrong? How can you say you believe the same as he? Listen to his warning:

> Let us not bring in deceitful balances, to which we may hang what weights we will and how we will, saying to suit ourselves, "This is heavy and this is light;" but let us bring forward the sacred balance out of holy Scripture, as out of the Lord's treasure-house, and let us weigh them by it, to see which is the heavier; or rather, let us not weigh them for ourselves, but read the weights as declared by the Lord.[29]

These words confirm the Scriptures as the balance by which anything else is measured, just as I believe. Don't you think Augustine would want his own teachings held to the very same standard?

ROBERT: I'm sure he would say so.

JOSHUA: I'm sure he would too, which is why I test all of the early writers, and anyone else—including the Reformers— by the same standard. Augustine felt very strongly about this, seemingly believing that the Bible was so complete, so sufficient, that he could paraphrase Paul's apostolic warning of condemnation of false teaching[30] in these words:

> If anyone preaches either concerning Christ or concerning His church or concerning any other matter which pertains to our faith and life; I will not say, if we, but what Paul adds, if an angel from heaven should preach to you anything besides what you have received in the Scriptures of the Law and of the Gospels, let him be anathema.[31]

---

[29] *On Baptism, Against the Donatists,* II:6.
[30] From Galatians 1:8–9.
[31] *Contra litteras Petiliani,* 3:6.

Think of what is said here! Paul anathematized anyone who would preach a gospel other than the one he preached. But Augustine, writing less than four centuries later, evidently believed that the "Scriptures of the Law and the Gospels" embodied the very same standard that would allow the pronouncement of the anathema upon false gospels. Doesn't this seemingly indicate that there is nothing in "tradition" necessary for a true knowledge of the gospel itself? As Augustine said elsewhere:

> For though the Lord Jesus did many such acts, yet all of them are not recorded; just as this same St. John the evangelist himself testifies, that Christ the Lord both said and did many things that are not recorded; but such were chosen for record as seemed to suffice for the salvation of believers.[32]

Robert: Of *course* the simple gospel message is found in Scripture, Joshua—no one argues otherwise.

JOSHUA: But is *everything* you need to know for salvation clearly propounded in Scripture, Robert? I reject the bodily assumption of Mary. I reject the dogma of the Immaculate Conception and the infallibility of the pope and purgatory and a number of other such doctrines—I would say they are all extra-scriptural as well. So I believe that, taken consistently, Augustine's views of authority would provide me with a basis for the rejection of those teachings; indeed, one could argue that outside of a vague concept of purgation, Augustine did not believe in the things I just listed either. Let me close with one of my favorite quotes from Augustine:

> All things that are read from the Holy Scriptures in order to our instruction and salvation, it behooves us to hear with earnest heed. . . . And yet even in regard of them (a thing which ye ought especially to observe, and to commit to your memory, because that which shall make us strong against insidious errors, God has been pleased to put in the Scriptures, against which no man dares to speak, who in any sort wishes to seem a Christian), when He had given Himself to be handled by them, that did not suffice Him, but He would also confirm

---

[32] *Tractates on John*, XLIX, John 11:1–54.

by means of the Scriptures the heart of them that believe: for He looked forward to us who should be afterwards; seeing that in Him we have nothing that we can handle, but have that which we may read.[33]

Now compare these tremendous words with those of Jesuit founder Ignatius Loyola, writing more than eleven centuries later:

That we may be altogether of the same mind and in conformity with the Church herself, if she shall have defined anything to be black which to our eyes appears to be white, we ought in like manner to pronounce it black.[34]

That, Robert, is one of the clearest examples of *sola ecclesia* I've ever seen, and it contrasts strongly with what we have observed in other citations. You began by saying my understanding of biblical supremacy and sufficiency could not be correct because no one believed in it before the Reformation. Well, I believe I have solid basis for questioning *and* rejecting your assertion, and I suggest to you that the viewpoints expressed by the most solid, well-read, balanced writers indicates a significantly different understanding.

---

[33] *Ten Homilies on the First Epistle of John,* Homily 2, 1 John 2:12–17, sect. 1.
[34] Ignatius Loyola, "Rules for Thinking With the Church," Rule 13, cited from *Documents of the Christian Church,* ed., Henry Bettenson (Oxford, 1947), 364–65.

Conclusion: Forever Settled in Heaven . . . and for Me

I n this work we have barely scratched the surface of *sola scriptura*. Even so, as I said from the start, my goal truly has been to kindle a fire in the hearts of God's people, not only for His Word but for the *sufficiency* of His Word.

I have often preached that Christ is a perfect Savior, that He possesses the power and the nature to save without fail, and that He will share His glory with no other. I have used these truths as a basis upon which to exhort believers to rejoice in Christ's *sufficiency*. Look to Him for your every need! Do not allow the world to distract you, to draw you away so as to nibble at the worthless crumbs the world would offer you rather than dine at the Lord's Table, where there is enough spiritual food and drink to satiate the strongest desires. We have a *sufficient* Savior, fully capable of doing what the Father has willed Him to do (John 6:38–39).

In the very same way, our Lord Jesus Christ has provided His Word to His bride, the church. The Word is His voice, and He has chosen to speak with clarity and with sufficiency. He has given this tremendous gift out of love, for He has protected it and blessed those who have remained faithful to its teachings. Its sufficiency is a great encouragement to His people, for without it they would be left wandering in darkness, always casting about for some other source to guide them to the truth in the kind of certainty needed for a life of godliness and service in a hostile world.

The God-breathed Scriptures speak to every generation of believers with the same soul-changing, truth-imparting power as they did from the beginning. The psalmist thrilled to the sufficiency and clarity of God's Word in Psalm 119, so how much more can believers in our day, who have such tremendous treasures as the gospel of John or the epistle to the Romans, revel in what He has given us? For the believer, the fact that God holds people accountable for what they read in Scripture is reason for rejoicing, for this means we have the privilege of hearing directly from God when we come humbly before His Word. While for the unbeliever this only brings judgment, since God has given us His Word and will hold us accountable to it, for the believer it is reason for celebration, a sure sign of His continued faithfulness to His promise to build His church and bless His people.

Some of the subjects we have addressed in this work—inspiration, inerrancy, canon, exegesis, allegations of corruption and contradiction—are considered *too difficult* to be discussed in today's comfortable church. And yet if we do not put forth the effort to master these areas, we cannot claim to have a real and valid faith in the Scriptures. Instead, our faith becomes sentimentality, our conviction mere opinion or predilection, and our message lost in the myriad voices clamoring for people's attention. When we hold firmly to God's truth, work through the difficult issues and challenges, and become clear in our understanding of the whys and the wherefores, we can truly say, without fear and without embarrassment, "God has said this in His Holy Word."

This world has become an indescribably challenging place. Issues of ethics and morality, extending from abortion through genetic experimentation, euthanasia, homosexuality, and the complete redefinition of the divine institution of marriage and family are all around us. Postmodernism has destroyed the foundation of truth, humanism has annihilated the highest and best in man, and naturalistic materialism has banished hope from his mind. The world has nothing to offer him, since he is created in the image of God, and so he lives in constant rebellion against this nature and the testimony of God's existence all around him and within him. Only Christ's church, blessed with His Word, can speak to his truest needs. The enemy, knowing this, attacks the Scriptures in every conceivable fashion, seeking to sow seeds of doubt in believers' minds so that they will not boldly proclaim to the world the very truths God's Word has revealed.

This is why you, my fellow believer, must not put this book down and say, "Ah, I have accomplished my task, I may now move on to other things." Again, this is a primer, a beginning, a start. I noted a number of works in the introduction that go far beyond the scope of this present volume, and into much more depth. With this foundation you will be able to appreciate their wealth of information and utilize it more effectively. Hopefully my own passion for these truths will be evident to you and encourage you to press through some of the more challenging portions of those works.

But even if you do not pursue those resources, it is truly my prayer that you will stop and thank God the next time you place your hand upon your Bible. That you will realize how special it is and how much of a testament it is to God's love for you, believer in Jesus Christ. And I hope you will take the time to sit down and ponder the passages of Scripture we could only lightly touch upon, meditate upon their richness, and see that their testimony is repeated endlessly throughout the pages of Holy Scripture.

I shared early on that I grew up in a Christian family. From my youth I have known the words to the great hymn "How Firm a Foundation." It is a theme song for me, a motto, a reminder of the love God has placed in my heart for His Word. It is a fitting conclusion to our study.

How firm a foundation, ye saints of the Lord,
Is laid for your faith in His excellent Word!
What more can He say than to you He hath said,
To you who for refuge to Jesus have fled? [1]

---

[1] "How Firm a Foundation," lyrics by John Rippon, 1787; music by Joseph Funk, 1832.

Scripture Index

More Foundational Theology
From James White

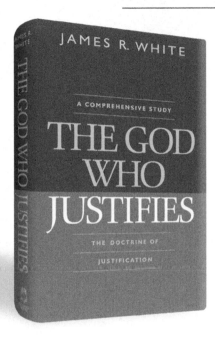

A Comprehensive Study
of the Doctrine of Justification

The history of the Christian church pivots on the doctrine of justification by faith. Once the core of the Reformation, the church today often ignores or misunderstands this foundational doctrine. Theologian James White calls believers to a fresh appreciation of, understanding of, and dedication to the great doctrine of justification and then provides an exegesis of the key Scripture texts on this theme.

The God Who Justifies

Recovering the Heart of Christian Belief

In *The Forgotten Trinity* we are brought back into the presence of the Godhead in a way that will affect how we view God's character and change our worship. Faced with the mystery of the Trinity, we are left with two options: willful ignorance or a deeper understanding of the awesome God that presents himself to us.

The Forgotten Trinity

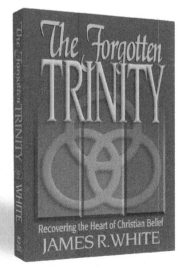

BETHANYHOUSE